THE LUIGI WAY

THE LUIGI WAY

BENEDICTINE VALUES PROVEN EFFECTIVE IN LEADERSHIP

LOUIS DONATO TATE

NEW DEGREE PRESS

THE LUIGI WAY

Benedictine Values Proven Effective in Leadership

ISBN   979-8-88504-120-1 *Paperback*
         979-8-88504-749-4 *Kindle Ebook*
         979-8-88504-228-4 *Ebook*

To my loving family, staff, and Luigi's patrons. This book would not have been possible without you.

Table of Contents

Introduction

"Culture does not change because we desire it to change. Culture changes when the organization is transformed; the culture reflects the realities of the people working together every day."
—FRANCES HESSELBEIN

The restaurant industry statistically has one of the highest failure rates of all industries. According to an article published by *CNBC* in March of 2016, 60 percent of restaurants fail within the first year and 80 percent of restaurants fail within the first five years of business. The industry's volatility poses multiple risks and challenges both seen and unforeseen that restaurant owners both new and seasoned must constantly be conscious of while trying their best to be prepared for whatever may happen.

But restaurants aren't the only industry with a high failure rate. Other businesses suffer as well, and you might be surprised about the reason for this. After talking to other business owners and conducting some of my own independent research, I found the most common causes for failure in business are linked back to toxic values in the workplace's culture. Each of the following qualities are common causes for failure in all businesses. Those include:

- **Absentee Ownership**: Not being a "hands-on" owner, working alongside your team, setting a good example of your culture's values from the top.
- **The Values of the Culture Are Not Clear or Emphasized:** If you are in the highest position of leadership, it is essential to the health and longevity of your business that your staff is fully aware of the morals and values your organization is based on. You must have people within your organization who not only know them, but also believe in them.
- **Training of Managers and Other Leaders Within the Organization Is Poor or Inconsistent:** People in these positions should be a mirror of you and must reflect the values and morals you want to embed into your culture. Sustainability of these must start from the top. If not, it can lead to confusion, lack of motivation and commitment, and high turnover.
- **Inadequate Allocation of Resources:** Ownership or management allowing their physical, financial, emotional, and human resources to go underused or undervalued. They are not mindful of the needs of their business, their team, or the community they serve, focusing more on their own personal needs before the needs of their business.
- **Poor Customer Service:** Management and staff are inconsistent in the services they provide. Staff or management not placing the needs of the customer first paired with no consistency in correcting customer's poor experience or not making an effort to make it right to the customer.

- **Failure to Properly Vet Applicants/Hiring Staff Who Don't Fit the Culture:** Similar to the explanation in the previous bullet point, hiring staff who do not fit your organization's culture not only negatively affects your current staff, but the customers who keep your business alive. Creating unnecessary tension within the culture can lead to higher employee turnover and loss of business from customers.

- **Communication within the Organization Only Flows from the Top to the Bottom:** It is essential for an organization to have communication shared from top to bottom and bottom to top. As I like to tell my staff and customers, I as the manager/owner-operator primarily oversee the operations of the moving parts of the business and ensure everything is moving in the right direction. But it is my staff in each of those departments that identify more micro-level details of their job and how they perform it. It is crucial to the business/organization's success that they give feedback and input regarding current problems and possible solutions. Think of communication as watering a plant. When a plant is deprived of water, it becomes droopy, fades in color, and overall doesn't look healthy. Water restores its health and well-being.

- **Prioritizing Only the Needs of the Business and Not the Needs of Your Staff:** Every business or organization has both a human and operational side to it. Both require a balanced focus. Your staff are human beings, not robots. They have emotions and are susceptible to mental and physical limitations and challenges. It is crucial that leaders have an open ear to the needs and concerns of their team. If their needs aren't being met, the needs of your organization will not be met.

So how did a restaurant in a small town with one red light survive not only the challenges of COVID-19, but thirty-eight years of challenges and hardships? The answer is quite simple. Building, maintaining, and sustaining a healthy work culture. A healthy culture is the lifeline supporting any business and is ultimately the root cause of a business or organization's success or failure. The fundamental characteristic of a healthy workplace's culture is credited to having a strong set of values embedded into the organization's culture—values everyone who belongs to that organization shares and that serve as the "why" to a business or organization's existence, actions, and mission.

An idea that turned into a destination— little did my father, Louis Tate, and his brother, Edward Tate, realize what their restaurant would evolve into.

My family's business, known as Luigi's Ristorante, began when my father and my uncle were looking for their calling. The two of them collectively put their savings together and took out a loan (with nothing to back it) and purchased an old tavern in the small town of Clymer, Pennsylvania in 1984. The tavern's layout included a main dining area with a handful of mismatched tables and chairs, a horseshoe-shaped bar, and a tiny side dining room with ten more small tables. The kitchen was roughly a little over two hundred square feet.

The building could sit approximately seventy people at once. When I asked my father about the first thing they did when preparing to open, he shared that he remembers talking to his brother, Ed, and his father, Skip, about how they first needed to give the building a deep clean and utilize whatever equipment was left there when they first bought the building. There was no excess capital at the time to update the facilities the way they desired to.

When they first opened, the menu was very small. They only offered a few sandwiches, such as meatball and hot sausage subs, soups, salads, and a few pasta dishes such as lasagna, spaghetti, and fettuccine alfredo. The kitchen was so small that my grandmother, Barbara, made the lasagna for the day at her house and brought it to the restaurant. My grandfather, along with two other experienced cooks, did the cooking in the restaurant to start. Everyone working for the business in the beginning was family except the two experienced cooks they hired, whom they still viewed as family.

The generational faith-based values they learned from their parents, paired with the work ethic they learned while working for their family's grocery store, has resulted in and continues to fuel the expansive growth of their business and leadership skills. Over the last thirty-eight years, we have expanded into four locations: Luigi's Ristorante & Catering in Clymer and DuBois, Pennsylvania, Luigi's Pizzeria in Clymer, and Luigi's Villa Banquet Facility in DuBois. In addition, we currently sell our jarred spaghetti sauce in multiple grocery stores throughout western and northern Pennsylvania.

Since I was ten years old, I have been involved in my family's restaurant. Working from the ground up, I am now part-owner of Luigi's Ristorante & Pizzeria in Clymer, Pennsylvania. From cleaning toilets and dishes, to cooking, serving, and management, I have learned powerful lessons on the importance of leadership and what it takes to be an effective leader. The mentorship of my parents, relatives, co-workers, college professors, priests, and customers has played a critical role in my development as a leader. Without them, I would not be the same leader I am today.

My brother Salvatore (ten) and I (fourteen) working on a busy Sunday afternoon. Now that we're older, we are grateful for the opportunity to develop a work ethic at such a young age. This experience has benefited us in every aspect of our lives.

There is one specific leadership lesson my father instilled in me at a young age. "To be leader, you must be willing to step up, take charge, and get done whatever needs to be done, especially when others won't. To be an effective leader, you must be willing to get in the trenches and do the hard work, be hands-on, communicate and coordinate with your team, make them feel involved and appreciated. Be willing to admit your mistakes and learn from others. That is when you will truly earn their trust and respect."

Throughout my life, whether it be my involvement in the family businesses, sports teams, clubs, classes, and volunteer work, I have always found myself in a position of leadership. In that position of leadership, I learned to not be afraid of failure. To embrace failure, and let that failure be a benchmark for improvement, led me closer to success. Though each organization has its differences, they all have one thing in common: A lifeline is dependent on its culture and its values. I have been in healthy cultures and toxic cultures. In both instances, there was always a lesson to be learned and something to be improved.

The most important lesson I have learned throughout these experiences is the success of any organization is based on the health and shared interests of the individuals within that organization. That health is maintained by the values the business is built on and values the whole team shares in. You can have the most attractive product or services, but if you do not have a healthy culture reflecting the values of yourself and the other people within that organization, the organization becomes unsustainable and succumbs to failure.

This book will focus on the importance of how to build, sustain, and maintain a healthy culture within an organization. My hope is this book will help and/or challenge how you view leadership and the importance of having it paired with a strong set of values, and how having a strong set of values in your workplace culture can ensure long-term success. By doing so, I will share with you the value system embedded into the cultural fabric of my family's business and how it has helped us overcome any challenge or form of adversity we have faced, particularly COVID-19.

In addition, I will share stories and examples from myself, my family and relatives, customers, and employees both past and present on how we have lived by these values and how they have fueled our success. You will read insights from psychologists, business leaders, professors, and other writers who focus on leadership skills and development. In a world where we are told what to think, this book is created with the intention to *make* you think, to help you take stock of your own life, and how you, the reader, can apply and implement these values into your organization's culture to help ensure success in any challenge, both seen and unforeseen.

CHAPTER 1

Our Origins

"All people have is hope. That's what brings the next day and whatever that day may bring...a hope grounded in the real world of living, friendship, work, family."

—BRUCE SPRINGSTEEN

The year was 1984. My father, Louis, was a blink away from turning thirty years old. Certain life circumstances troubled him and left him unsure of what his future held and what he was destined to be. My father always had aspirations of being an entrepreneur but wasn't certain what kind. All he knew was he wanted to be in business for himself. Then, with no warning, an unanticipated opportunity presented itself and launched the beginning of what's known today as Luigi's Ristorante.

WHAT CREATED THE ENTREPRENEURIAL VISION
My father has always envisioned himself as an entrepreneur. It was one of his dreams. He was the son, grandson, and great-grandson of entrepreneurs. His great-grandfather,

Salvatore Teti, an Italian immigrant, came to the United States in hopes of a better living for himself and a brighter future for his next generation of family. Salvatore and his family ended up in Wilkes-Barre Scranton, Pennsylvania in the late 1800s before moving to a small coal town named Arcadia with intentions of working in the coal mines.

Shortly after moving to the area, he noticed a demand for a store that sold coal miner supplies and other general grocery items such as dairy and meat, as well as convenience items. It was then in 1905 he opened his own store, naming it "Tate Brothers." Shortly before the Great Depression hit, he passed away from unknowingly rupturing his appendix, leaving behind his wife, Anina, and their three children.

During The Great Depression, my family's grocery store was temporarily shut down, like many other businesses in the area, let alone the nation. Not long after that, Anina moved to my hometown of Clymer, Pennsylvania, eleven miles away from Arcadia. Shortly after, she purchased a small family-owned grocery store. With the help of her two sons, Anthony (my great-grandfather) and Albert, they continued to operate Tate's Supermarket, which is still in operation to this day, 117 years later. After some time and consideration, Albert decided to move toward Newcastle, Pennsylvania, leaving ownership of the store to his brother. Anthony had three sons who eventually became part of the ownership. Their names were Anthony, William "Skip" Salvatore (my grandfather), and George.

The original Tate's store once they relocated to Clymer, PA.
Pictured from left to right is Anthony P. Tate (my great grandpa),
Mary Tate (Anthony's sister), Joe Tate (Anthony's cousin).

At the age of ten, my father began working at the family
supermarket. He was tasked with stocking shelves and
unloading trucks, labor intensive tasks that instilled a work
ethic at a young age. My grandpa and his brothers were your
typical mid-1900s business owners with the mentality of
"work, work, work...and when you think you're done working,
you work some more." Growing up working in a family business came with many sacrifices and lessons. The only time
my father got off work was for weddings and funerals. He
sacrificed his weekends and social life to support the business
with aspirations of being one of the owners one day. He did
not have the childhood and young adult life like his friends
did and he would've liked to have had. Being the oldest of
seven children and the leader, his mind was set on becoming
part-owner of the grocery store like his father.

After working in the grocery store for twenty years, he came to the realization that things were different now compared to when his father and two uncles were single men without any children to support. The supermarket was already supporting three families, and as the new heir of owners began to have their own, things could become complicated, thus strengthening his vision of starting his own business. At thirty years old, he knew it was time to make a move. But the question in his mind was, "What is this move going to be, and when will the right opportunity arise?"

THE FOUNDING OF LUIGI'S RISTORANTE

The year was 1984. My uncle Ed can remember the night when my father and grandfather had a life-changing conversation. My father was puzzled, having realized that after years of sacrifice and commitment to the family business, it was not going to be his destiny. The emotions of curiosity, speculation, and fear weighed on his heart. Having not gone to college, the thought of not having many other options seemed real. Most people would give way to these emotions, but not my father. Having faith in God at the forefront of his focus, and a strong work ethic instilled in him at a young age, he knew if he kept his faith strong and didn't doubt himself, something great would come from this. As my father and grandfather continued brainstorming, my grandfather mentioned how a miner's tavern named Angie's (formerly known as Benamati's) was for sale. He said, "Why don't we buy it and get you your own business?" That was the night his life changed forever.

Shortly after, Uncle Ed returned home from working in the mines and overheard my father and grandfather's conversation. "I started thinking, I was always close with my brother. I was close enough that I said to him, 'Hey, if there's room for me, I'd like to be a part of that someday. I don't want to be in the coal mines the rest of my life.'"

My father agreed and quickly realized it was much better to own your own business (or own it with your brother) starting from scratch with the same goals and mindset, than to work in a family business with multiple owners who were not immediate family. Not long after this conversation, the idea became a reality. My father and uncle went to Marion Center Bank located seven miles away in Marion Center, PA, and took out a loan for fifty-two thousand dollars to buy the building. The president of the bank, Richard Oberlin, knew our family very well, further influencing his decision to allow them to borrow the whole amount with no down payment and no collateral in case things didn't work out. The only reason they were approved for the loan was because of their family's good reputation and spotless credit. The bank president took a chance and agreeably lent them the money they needed to buy the old tavern.

Before Uncle Ed had teamed up with my father, he worked in the coal mines. When he graduated high school, he believed my father was destined to be the only immediate family member to have an ownership in the family supermarket, so he decided to go to trade school for mine mechanics. At the time, the coal industry was one of the dominant and highest paying industries for working class people not only in Pennsylvania, but in the entire Northeastern part of the

United States. Knowing this, it seemed like the "golden ticket" opportunity at the time. But after seven years of swing shifts and dangerous work conditions, he felt it was time for a change. Timing is everything, and it seemed like it was the perfect time and opportunity to make the change they both so desperately needed and desired.

After purchasing the building, they both unanimously agreed to make their new business a restaurant/bar just like its previous owner. The main difference was they wanted to introduce an Italian menu to the area and transition it into a restaurant geared toward serving families rather than a tavern. They knew this place was going to need to work. The tavern was very small and decently furnished—enough to get them started. There were a few mixed and matched sets of plates, silverware, table clothes, cups, tables and chairs in the bar area, a horseshoe bar, and an L-shaped dining room with around twelve tables. The kitchen was approximately a little over two hundred square feet empty.

After they added some basic kitchen appliances like a single burner stove, an oven, a grill, a single-door refrigerator and a single door freezer, a pizza oven, a sink, counter space, and some utensils, there wasn't much room to walk around. Anyone working had to squeeze past one another sideways to get by. The bar was musty, and the bathroom reeked of urine and booze. They knew this was going to be a massive undertaking to renovate this building and give it the face lift it desperately needed. They began by giving it a thorough cleaning from top to bottom, a new paint job, replacing some flooring, adding some carpeting, and a new HVAC system and didn't do another thing until it was paid off. Starting a small family business from scratch, they didn't want to overextend themselves and take on more debt than they already had—especially not knowing if it would succeed or not. Incrementally over time, they completed one renovation project after another, until the required improvements, big and small, were eventually completed.

A photo taken by the *Indiana Gazette* in an article written in 1987 about Clymer. Pictured from left to right is Uncle Ed, Great-Grandfather Anthony, and Dad Louie.

When I asked my Aunt Teresa about what she remembered when my father and uncle first bought the building and starting their business, she shared, "Well, I was at home and present physically for the many discussions that took place with my father and grandfather sitting at the dining room table, discussing for hours whether to purchase Benamati's building and start a restaurant. Grandfather Tate had owned a bowling alley/restaurant/dance hall in Medina, New York. He had first-hand knowledge and experience on the time, work, and effort put into a successful restaurant/business. I remember him saying to my father, 'A restaurant is the hardest business there is.' He had concerns and was not fully supportive of my father taking on this new endeavor. Understandable, with my father being fifty-five years old and contemplating taking out a loan for fifty-two thousand dollars and putting a lien against his home and the small house next door that my parents purchased after the Tatay family passed away," she continued. "But for my father, what really was the driving force all along was the fact he knew his mother's (Mary E. Perry Tate) recipes were ethnic and wonderfully delicious and he was excited to share the famous sauce and meatballs soon to become a favorite in Western, Pennsylvania. People come from all over to enjoy the sauce and pasta entrée."

Teresa added, "What really sticks out in my memory is the small, submarine-shaped kitchen. So elongated...I can see my father carrying a heavy boiling pot of pasta that needed to be drained in the colander and he had to squeeze past the other person to get to the sink...I can see my dad stirring the sauce with his apron on wanting everything to be cooked to his mother's recipes. He loved hearing compliments from the patrons. The aroma of the famous family sauce recipe simmering on the burner and meatballs being prepared was about to take over in full-blown aromatic scent. Just like our homestead every Sunday after attending mass/church, our family would feast along with our grandfather and grandmother on this delicious homemade sauce. The patrons were going to enjoy a traditional Italian pasta dinner like we did at home for years."

A current picture of our location in Clymer, PA. Now currently owned and operated by my dad, Louie, and myself. This picture was taken by Rev. Fr. Gregorio D. Soldevilla, Jr.

"Follow your passion, be prepared to work hard and sacrifice, and above all, don't let anyone limit your dreams."

—DONOVAN BAILEY

They quickly realized how difficult it was to start a business from scratch. The first and biggest challenge they faced was they had absolutely no experience or knowledge of the restaurant industry. For several years, their growth was driven by trial and error, making mistakes that became learning lessons and failures that became improvements. Spending many years working in the grocery store provided not just a strong work ethic, but also a business background and financial literacy—a mindset required to own and operate any type of business.

Arguably more important, having the moral and physical support of their parents and siblings was crucial to their success early on and even until this day. In the beginning stages of the business, Grandfather Skip, Grandmother Barbara, and two women who were self-taught chefs did all of the cooking; they used their own family recipes, handed down from their parents and grandparents, and made everything they served homemade, which we still do to this day.

My aunts helped serve customers as well as tend bar alongside my father and Uncle Ed. It was truly a family affair. My uncle kept his job in the coal mines, working countless hours at both the mines and the restaurant, further ensuring their business would succeed. They began with a simple one-page menu. This was at the suggestion of their parents. "Start with a simple menu. Don't attempt to do too much too fast. Give yourselves time to work out the kinks, then slowly begin to add more items to the menu and more staffing as it permits."

My grandfather, William "Skip" Tate, preparing some food. He loved cooking for people.

They thought they had sacrificed a lot working in the supermarket, but that was miniscule compared to the financial, social, and physical sacrifices they had to make now. This kind of sacrifice required giving up time with family and friends, working on holidays, working dawn to dusk, canceling plans, and not have much take-home pay. It required them to spend fourteen to sixteen hours a day, seven days a week, serving breakfast, lunch, and dinner and even late nights with the bar open after the dining room closed to build the business—not because they wanted to, but because they had to. With no investors or large capital reserve to comfort them, they knew they had to make every minute and penny matter. Not only was it a sacrifice for them, but also their parents and siblings who wanted them to be successful just as much as they did. They knew this was their calling and they were driven to be successful.

With demand slowing growing day by day, year by year, it allowed them the opportunity to employ some extra staff. They hired a couple cooks, bartenders, servers, and dish washers. In addition, they finally achieved their desire to chip away at more of the interior and exterior projects such as replacing all of the windows, purchasing matching tables, chairs, and table clothes, replacing the roof, adding new appliances, expanding the size of the kitchen, and adding an outdoor seating area.

The cosmetic upgrades they made gave the old building a new look, gradually forming it's new identity. Slowly but surely, they created the business they envisioned. As things progressed, my father approached his father with the idea of closing on Sundays. My grandfather quickly responded, "Bullshit! You're staying open seven days a week for breakfast, lunch, and dinner until the mortgage is paid off. Then after that, you can start to think about taking it a little easier."

My grandfather was a tough guy and a hard-working, faith-filled man who understood the importance of work, integrity, and community. Even though it was my father and uncle's business, their father was still the boss. Every decision they made was ran by him out of respect—respect for his opinion and his wisdom. Having been an entrepreneur his whole life, they understood the importance of his contribution to their business. As challenging as things got at times, neither my uncle nor my father had any moments of regret. They both admitted they believe they didn't realize what they had gotten themselves into at the time, but they were determined to make it work and wanted to show their parents they were going to make it.

BUILDING THE CULTURE THEY ENVISIONED
A few years into the business, their sales and reputation steadily increased and expanded. They began to get a better feel for things and had more confidence in the future. There was still one pressing factor that required their constant attention: transforming the atmosphere of the old business into the atmosphere they desired to create for their clientele. For many years, the building was known as a place where patrons could carry on and have more than a few drinks, expressing whatever provocative beliefs or thoughts were on their mind; your typical bar scene.

Their goal was to turn this business's atmosphere into one warm and welcoming. A culture that would embrace family feelings and values where families could bring their children without worrying about being exposed to anything inappropriate. To do this, they understood it was going to take time. They had to have constant awareness and attentiveness to potential or present conflicts and maintain law and order. They had a zero-tolerance policy for abusing alcohol and profanity, resulting in the attraction and retention of the kind of clientele they wished to serve: families. To do this, they needed to be consistent in:

- Respectfully defining what their values, morals, and "non-negotiable" behaviors are (what is permitted/ expected and what is not) to their staff.
- Strategically building a culture based on those desired values, morals, and expected behaviors. Putting in place checks and balances ensuring accountability.
- Maintaining a constant focus that our culture and our brand are aligned with each other.
- Most importantly, living up to their values by their actions and developing a team of people who share in those values.

It took my father and uncle roughly five years to change the building's former reputation of a tavern to a casual fine dining family restaurant. Sticking to this goal, they achieved it. They conquered one of many initial challenges, knowing there were more to come.

OPPORTUNITY FOR EXPANSION
Roughly five years after opening, my father saw an opportunity to open another business. Another old building located

near the restaurant came up for sale. At first, they were skeptical about taking on another mortgage payment only five years after opening the first. The more thought they put into it, the more intrigued my father became. It was a stately old building with character, it was well maintained, and had an ideal location, being only one hundred feet away from the main traffic light in town. The light bulb went off, and my father said to Ed and their father, "Why don't we buy it and open a pizza shop?" My uncle was supportive and saw the long-term benefits. If they continued to work as hard as they had with the restaurant, they could build the pizza shop to the point where they could have employees helping them run it to lighten the workload they already had. Of course, they understood this would come with even greater sacrifice.

Being young and ambitious, they decided to buy it and open a pizzeria. Shortly after opening, my grandfather adamantly lamented to my father, "Why did you buy that building? You are already devoting all of your time to this restaurant. How do you plan to balance both?" He was frustrated because he initially thought they made a mistake, but my father saw the bigger picture. Not only did this building have a prime location, but it was right beside a movie rental store. For years, he noticed how many people constantly went in and out of that movie store. He believed having a pizza shop conveniently located right beside it would inevitably be successful. "What a perfect combination: picking up a movie and a pizza all within a few steps," my father said. Surely enough, he was right, and that's exactly what happened. After that, my grandfather finally quit giving my father hell.

My father vividly remembers a conversation he had with his father during the first year or two of operating the pizza shop. He shared, "My father would frequently ask me out of curiosity, 'How's that place doing down there?' I would always respond, 'Okay,' and that was it. After several attempts to get a more in-depth answer, my father asked me, 'Are you sure you're not taking any money from the restaurant to pay the bills for the pizza shop?' I responded, 'Not yet!'"

A current picture of our pizza shop, Luigi's Pizzeria. This picture was taken by Rev. Fr. Gregorio D. Soldevilla, Jr.

OUR FIRST MAJOR SETBACK

In 1996, twelve years after opening the restaurant, my father and uncle experienced their first major setback. On the day I was born, my father left the hospital full of joy, only to find his business on fire. An electrical fire started in the kitchen of the building. The entire back end of the restaurant was engulfed in flames. Black smoke flooded the sky with embers lighting up the sky like stars. He was in total disbelief. Fortunately, the firefighters kept the fire under control and prevented total damage to the whole building. The areas of the restaurant not affected by the fire did suffer damage from the smoke. To this day, there are still several pictures hanging in the restaurant that were in the restaurant during the time of the fire with black smoke stains on them.

This situation presented a tough decision for my father and uncle: Option one was to close the restaurant for an unknown amount of time until the building was repaired, and option two was closing the restaurant permanently and sell the building. With both men now having children, the decision was tougher than ever anticipated. After putting time and consideration into this critical decision, they quickly decided they would repair the damages and reopen. Having the pizza shop and a second form of income made this decision a little easier, but they knew it could be challenging to sustain two families on this tiny business's income. By the grace of God, the pizza shop supported both of their families for six months until they reopened the restaurant.

Scene from Luigi's '96 April fire

Although the restaurant's staff was temporarily laid off, every single one of them returned to work as soon as we reopened. This was a testament to how my father and uncle treated their staff. They could've easily stayed working elsewhere and chose not to return to Luigi's, but to the staff, it was an easy decision to return to work.

Without knowing what had happened the day before, one of our head chefs, Patricia Pavlosky, who's been with us for twenty-seven years and counting, showed up to work early in the morning the day after the fire and was shocked to see what had happened to her home away from home. "I couldn't wait to get back to cooking. It was what I lived for and didn't consider it a job. Cooking is what I love to do," Patricia said. She was the first person committed to coming back to work once we reopened and was excited to continue doing what she loves to do, especially in a brand-new kitchen! She shared, "I enjoy the rush of preparing some of our signature dishes, such as Beef Braciole, Pasta Fagioli soup, meatballs, lasagna, and many more. I was in my heaven hustling around the kitchen doing my thing: prepping hard as always and going above and beyond the call of duty."

Another staff member with us before the fire and who came back was one our other head chefs, Vickie Vennard, who's been with us for twenty-eight years and counting. When Vickie first heard the restaurant had caught on fire over the radio, her response to hearing the news was, "I was nervous about being out of work, but also thought that sometimes things come to us through tragedies. I was now able to help my mother-in-law with her health complications until we reopened."

A few days after the fire, Vickie received a call from my father. He reassured her that her job would still be there if she was willing to come back. After a long six months, the restoration and renovations of Luigi's was finally complete. At that time, Vickie was working at another restaurant. Once Luigi's reopened, Vickie decided to leave her temporary job to come back. "Luigi's is family, and I missed that family," Vickie said. Shortly after the fire, my father and uncle began to realize now, both having their own families to support, they should expand and continue to build upon their growing success. But the question was how and when. At that time, there weren't any practical opportunities present until Divine Intervention opened the door to the next chapter of the Luigi's dynasty.

OPPORTUNITY FOR EXPANSION: PART TWO

Dr. Jeffrey Rice, a young dentist and investor from DuBois, Pennsylvania, had a vision to turn a dilapidated downtown DuBois into a prosperous attraction with open storefronts along the entire main street. Dr. Rice was a huge fan of Luigi's. Not only did he love the food, but more importantly, he appreciated the work ethic of my father and uncle and the way they operated their business. One day, Dr. Rice approached them and asked if they would ever consider opening another restaurant in DuBois. Dr. Rice knew their business had brand recognition in a multi-county radius, fueling his confidence that introducing a good, homemade Italian cuisine to downtown DuBois could be a huge success.

My father and uncle were intrigued. As attractive as it seemed, they had a tough decision to make. Not only would they have to start a second restaurant from scratch in a city located roughly fifty miles away, but it would result in them no longer sharing the workload and responsibilities of the first restaurant and pizza shop. They knew one of them would have to move to DuBois, but who? Considering my father was recently married and had a newborn child, all while building a house, it seemed only fitting that my uncle would move and spearhead this new business.

This decision resulted in some backlash and resistance from their parents. They didn't want them to open a third business at this point, arguing it would be too much to handle. Even back then, they knew the high risk of opening another restaurant. My grandfather told them not to do it. He said, "You're already working six to seven days a week. How can you handle more?" Even though they disagreed, their respect for their father's opinion led them to declining Dr. Rice's offer. Six months later, my grandfather passed away. During those months prior to his passing, two other restaurants accepted Dr. Rice's offer, but had trouble getting the necessary financing. Dr. Rice then contacted my father again and asked him to reconsider. My father said to my uncle, "I think it's a sign to have the same opportunity present itself twice." This time they told Dr. Rice yes. My father thought it was divine intervention.

After accepting Dr. Rice's offer, the business arrangements began. Considering my father and uncle did not have enough working capital to make this kind of massive investment solely on their own, Dr. Rice allowed them to lease-to-own the building. Once everything was paid for, they would completely own everything. Having helped start the original location in Clymer, Ed had a well-detailed list of everything he needed: everything from kitchen appliances, dining sets, tables, utensils, etc. He went to auctions to find the best deals he could. Before all of this came into play, they began with the complete remodeling of the interior and exterior building.

A photo taken of Uncle Ed and Dad shortly after opening their second location in DuBois, PA.

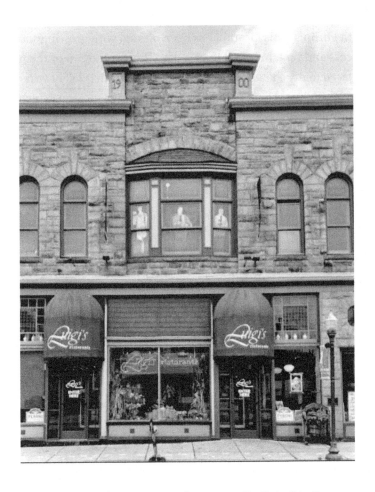

A current photo from our sister location in DuBois, PA. Currently owned and operated by my uncle Ed and cousin Mia.

After this, they hired a core group of staff, kitchen, and server managers to drive to Clymer several days a week to learn our current system. This business strategy decision was crucial to building and replicating the standardized business model that was successful at the original restaurant in Clymer. In 1999, they were prepared to open their doors for the first time in DuBois. This location has been blessed with growing success and remains open to this day. Though the two of them faced many challenges throughout the last thirty-eight years, nothing could have prepared them for March 19, 2020, which brought about the biggest unforeseen challenge they faced since their origins.

CHAPTER 2

March 19, 2020: (When COVID-19 Restrictions Hit Home)

———

"Coming together is a beginning. Keeping together is progress. Working together is success."

—HENRY FORD

With the odds already stacked against the industry, the mysterious COVID-19 virus began to rapidly spread throughout the world on January 9, 2020, taking only twelve days to reach the United States (AJMC, 2021).

As the surge of the virus continued to grow, COVID-19 became classified as a pandemic by the World Health Organization (WHO) on March 11, 2020 (AJMC, 2021). In an attempt to slow the spread of the virus, both federal and state governments imposed mandated lockdowns and restrictions on all "non-essential" businesses and organizations nationwide. With no clear idea of what threats this virus imposed and how long the lockdowns and restrictions would be enforced, there was no certainty on how and when we would get through these challenging times.

This virus introduced one of the biggest challenges the nation, and specifically the restaurant industry, has had to combat in modern history. In December of 2020, *Business Insider* released an article stating the statistics on how the COVID-19 lockdowns and restrictions impacted restaurants in the United States. In the article, a survey conducted by the National Restaurant Association found that since the beginning of the pandemic, 110,000 restaurants (about 17 percent of all restaurants) have permanently closed. Most of these restaurants weren't brand-new; the average business life of the restaurants that closed was sixteen years.

2019. A time many of us may refer to as "the old normal." The economy was booming. There were more jobs available than people to fill them, and businesses both large and small prospered. Going into 2020, we were excited and optimistic for what the new year would bring us. Little did we know, a little over three months into the new year, our entire value system would be tested as we were required to restructure our entire business operations overnight.

On January 9, 2020, WHO announced a "mysterious Corona-virus-related pneumonia" was discovered in Wuhan, China. This information quickly flooded all mainstream media and news outlets in the country. I remember having conversations with customers, staff, and friends about this new mysterious virus. None of us would have ever guessed this virus would plague the world like it did. It didn't take long for me and many others to realize this virus was here to stay, and today it is only getting stronger. Within the same month, the CDC confirmed the first case of COVID-19 in the United States—eventually leading to the WHO declaring a global health emergency and the United States declaring a public health emergency. The lack of public information on what this virus was, how it spread, and what to do to slow the spread left the general public confused and concerned. The only thing we knew was this virus was circulating rapidly through human transmission and taking lives around the world.

As confirmed cases of the virus continued to soar, statewide quarantines at the discretion of each state's governor went into effect. After the state of Pennsylvania saw its first confirmed case in March, Governor Wolf ordered schools to be closed for two weeks, sending millions of students home with intentions of slowing the spread and admission rates at hospitals. Only five days after this announcement, on Thursday, March 19, 2020, Governor Wolf announced all "non-life-sustaining businesses" were asked to close their businesses, following similar guidelines put in place in California and several other states. This mandate resulted in us temporarily closing on Friday, March 20, and reopening on the following Wednesday for takeout only service.

Governor Tom Wolf is quoted saying, "To protect the health and safety of all Pennsylvanians, we need to take more aggressive mitigation actions. This virus is an invisible danger that could be present everywhere. We need to act with the strength we use against any other severe threat. And we need to act now before the illness spreads more widely"

(Pennsylvania Government, 2020). Many people agreed with the governor's thoughts at the time. After hearing about this announcement, my father and I quickly researched the governor's list of businesses categorized as "life-sustaining" and "non-life-sustaining."

We were saddened to see restaurants were categorized as a "non-life-sustaining" business, but we were permitted to operate for takeout only services, which was better than being forced to completely close down. Due to these restrictions enforced the day after the announcement, we only had a few hours to strategize with our key staff members. Though none of us anticipated this kind of unforeseen challenge, and not having dealt with this kind of adversity before, we were confident that if we stuck together, worked together, and placed the needs of the well-being of our staff and customers first, we would get through this challenge.

Though it seemed there weren't many options or ideas on how to slow the spread of this mysterious virus, the governor's swift and aggressive actions came with some severe consequences. According to the *Philadelphia Inquirer*, federal data showed that when the restrictions on the state's labor force was enacted, almost 1.85 million or 28 percent of Pennsylvania's workforce filed for unemployment, soon to hit a record high of 6.9 million people on March 28, 2020. This was the beginning of a major ripple effect throughout our entire state and national economies.

Having no choice but to accept these new restrictions, we began with the smaller things we could control. The first thing we did was assess the schedule and decide who to temporarily release and who to keep employed. That was arguably one of the hardest, yet most necessary decisions we had to make. It is never easy to be in a position where you release someone from work, especially when you have no control over it. Transitioning from a full service dine-in, takeout, and catering business to takeout only required just one-fifth of our normal staff. We went from having an active staff of roughly sixty people for the restaurant in Clymer to about twelve.

Though a large fraction of our staff was temporarily laid off, we still made every effort we could to find some form of work for those who needed it. After receiving my call with the unfortunate news, Shelby Henry, one of our loyal servers for over twelve years, said, "I was very scared because I didn't want to lose my job. But I know Louis would be there for me. He kept me busy doing other jobs, odds and ends jobs, helping take orders, and answering the phone. I may not have been able to serve tables, but he was able to provide me with other work, so at least I still felt like I had a job until we were able to re-open for dine-in."

Prior to the pandemic, we were open six days a week with serving hours between nine to ten hours a day to only being open four days a week with serving hours between four to five hours a day. Prior to the pandemic, our average weekly takeout sales fluctuated between 5 to 8 percent of our total sales. Knowing this, we strategically rearranged our hours of operation to best fit when takeout orders were usually placed.

The thought process serving as our "why" for making this change to our hours of operation was dependent on two variables:

1. We studied the statistics on what timeframes our take-out sales saw the highest amount of volume (prior to the pandemic). Those stats were generated from our point-of-sale system.
2. Using these statistics gave us a gauge for when our busiest time for takeout orders were, allowing the opportunity to give us the best "bang for our buck" in anticipating that the volume of orders received would cover all of our operational expenses plus give us a little bit of an extra financial cushion incase another unforeseen problem arose, such as the compressor for our walk-in cooler needing replacement.

After completing this first challenging task, we began to meet with our key staff members to brainstorm ideas of how to change our operations to be adequately prepared for this new form of business. Everyone gave input based upon their specific job responsibilities, and getting said input was key to our success. Communication within the organization needs to flow from top to bottom and bottom to top, especially when making a critical operation change affecting the way the staff perform the job we hired them to do! Not only does this help make their job easier, it reassures them that their input is not only heard, but important to the longevity of the business they are loyal to.

One of our general managers, Daniel Patton, agreed! When the news of the restrictions first broke, we communicated our concerns with one another. Daniel mentioned, "Now being limited to takeout only, it is even more important all the hands that were in the pot were putting the same ingredients in and everyone knew from top to bottom and bottom to top, what needed to be done and when they needed to do it. Communication was key. All our work family here has the same goal, and that's to make sure we can do everything we can for our employees and our customers."

While meeting with Daniel, we discussed what our first steps to adapting to these changes. He suggested, "Making sure we knew what the restrictions were for the state of Pennsylvania, making sure we can comply with all of them so we could open safely, not just for our customers or for the guidelines put out by our state. That was the first thing that came to my mind. That just is getting all the information in our hands as much as we can right away." There was no warning of these restrictions and we had very limited time to adjust to them.

After checking the restrictions guidelines posted on the office of the governor's website and the guidelines posted on the CDC's website, we met with one of our main chefs, Shawn Arford. Shawn is both one of our prep chefs and our head line chef. We shared the information we had gathered that evening and brainstormed ideas of what operational changes had to be made in the kitchen. Shawn proposed, "We run a special promotion to clear out our inventory, and from there, develop a limited menu based on our best sellers, along with a gluten-free and meatless options. This limited menu will also help us with inventory control and mitigating waste."

After our discussions, we put together an action plan for adjusting to these restrictions. That action plan included several operational changes, including:

- Assigning one person designated to the cash drawer who handled cash transactions and helped answer the phone and greet customers. This person let the rest of the staff know who had arrived for their order.
- Assigning two other individuals to answer the phone and carry food out to vehicles or to the lobby, allowing for prompt and speedy service.
- Adding two expediters responsible for packaging takeout orders and ensuring all the food assigned to the order was correct, cutting down on the possibility of a mistake.
- Buying new heavy-duty plastic takeout containers that are microwave and dishwasher safe. These containers allowed food to stay fresh and hot for a longer duration of time while allowing the customer to put their food in the microwave in the same container if need be.
- Having two to three individuals in our salad department responsible for the preparing of salads, soups, and desserts. Having salads and dressing cups freshly prepared before opening in advance cut down on wait time for food orders.
- After creating a limited menu based on our best sellers, we had a massive special on a lot of our menu items to ensure no inventory went to waste. Fewer menu items meant less preparation times for orders. Our chefs provided us with a verbal guideline on how to properly space out takeout order times depending on their size and how many we had around the same time, helping to limit the kitchen bottlenecking as much as possible. This also helped us to serve our patrons promptly and efficiently.

- For the first time ever, we offered "heat and eat" entrees. Customers could simply buy their desired meal baked but cold with heating instructions at a discounted price. You would just simply call or show up, tell us how many meals you wanted, and you were on your way. Two meal package deals. Party trays of food, available hot or cold with heating instructions. This service was extremely beneficial to us and the customer since we were not permitted to be open for dine-in on Mother's Day, IUP Graduation, Father's Day, and Christmas Eve.
- We implemented additional safety and sanitation practices in accordance with the CDC guidelines to ensure all of our staff and patrons were safe.
- We offered curbside/contactless delivery and contactless payment.

A picture I took of our location in Clymer, PA, a couple months into takeout only services during the COVID-19 pandemic. Seeing this rainbow perfectly aligned over the restaurant was a sign to me from God that, when the storm of the pandemic was over, our business would survive.

Considering our geographic location, most of our clientele had to drive ten to twenty minutes to get to Luigi's. Driving that distance for dine-in was common but driving that distance or greater for takeout did not seem as likely, especially with the current state of the nation leaving us skeptical of how takeout only was going to go. As people self-quarantined and limited their expenses, we were surprised at the immense amount of support we received right from the beginning. People traveled from a tri-county radius, some even driving as far as an hour in one direction not just for our food, but because they did not want to see us go under and were willing to support however they could.

During this three-plus month period of takeout only services, several patrons ordered once a week every week. Some even ordered multiple times a week until we were permitted to reopen for partial dine-in services. Whether it was making a purchase of food or gift certificates, or even simply spreading the word about our restaurant or sharing and engaging with our posts on social media, we were grateful for every form of support we received. These forms of support helped carry us through the hardships of these temporary business restrictions. The Pizza Shop has always been takeout only, so nothing really changed there. In Clymer, being limited to takeout only forced not only changes to staffing, but many other operational changes as well.

We made sure we covered the finer details on how they perform their job, helping to further mitigate the possibility of a mistake or error, all with the intention of providing the best services we could in a timely manner. We felt confident in our adjustments and optimistic about the effectiveness and efficiency of these changes. Although it helped to have a game plan for being as best prepared as possible, ultimately, we knew going into this that we had to learn as we went. We collectively gave one another feedback, benchmarking our pros and cons of each business day, week, and month until we reached a point of operational excellence that had little to no defects. Even then, we continued those same practices. Our team understood going into this new COVID era of business we had to be open to continuous improvement, just as we have been prior to the pandemic.

The first month of takeout was definitely the most difficult. Some of the reasons why were due to having to make these major operational changes rapidly, not having customers dining in, having to temporarily lay off staff, the suspense of the possibility that one of your staff, friends, or family might contract the virus, and the economic uncertainty of the area as well as the state and nation, having to limit our hours of operation, not knowing how long this was going to last, and if this form of business would be sustainable enough to ensure our survival. It is safe to say we were all anxious and nervous, yet optimistic and confident in our staff, our product, our services, and our customer base that we would all pull through this. No matter the challenges we faced, we came out of this stronger and better equipped to accommodate the needs of our staff and our patrons.

One of our customers who's been one of our biggest supporters since our origins in 1984 is Scott Bassaro. Scott and his family have always chosen Luigi's to host any family event, birthday, graduation, and religious celebrations as well as frequently dine in or pick up takeout orders. When first hearing the news of the restrictions imposed on restaurants, Scott said, "I was fine knowing that all state and national protocols, as well as customer safety, would be top priority at Luigi's." During this period, Scott ordered takeout every Friday night and occasionally an additional weeknight takeout order. We are eternally grateful for him and our loyal patrons who supported us during those challenging times.

One night when Scott picked up his order, he mentioned, "Having a sister and brother-in-law in the Italian restaurant industry in San Francisco, I understand there is much time and daily efforts involved are a challenge even in the best of times, but to operate during the COVID-19 era is just hard to fathom." We appreciated him understanding the difficulties of those current times and shared with him what we were doing to adapt to these challenges. When I asked Scott for his feedback on our services, he said, "I appreciated how you simplified your menu to better meet demand, as well as upgrading your takeout containers to a top-notch microwave-safe container. They helped keep my food hot and secure while transporting it home. There was never a disappointment."

Looking back on this today, it amazes me the support our local community gave to not just our business, but all businesses in the area affected by these restrictions, especially after reading the statistics of how many restaurants have succumbed to permanent closures due to their inability to overcome the challenges created by the restrictions imposed on restaurants due to the spread of the virus. According to an article released by The National Restaurant Association on September 14, 2020 (about six months after the first shutdowns of restaurants in the US), "Nearly one in six restaurants (representing nearly 100,000 restaurants) is closed either permanently or long-term; nearly three million employees are still out of work; and the industry is on track to lose $240 billion in sales by the end of the year."

Another article published by Avery Hartmans on December 7, 2020, from *Business Insider* provides us with the most recent data available on these statistics. The article stated that The National Restaurant Association sent a letter to congress sharing the results of a nationwide survey they conducted assessing "the economic plight of restaurants." A direct quote from the article states, "The survey found that since the onset of the pandemic, 17 percent of US restaurants—or about 110,000 establishments—have permanently closed down, with 10,000 closing in the last three months alone. The majority of restaurants closed were not brand-new businesses, the association found: on average, they'd been in business for sixteen years."

Almost a year and a half after the COVID-19 restrictions went into effect, United States business owners both large and small are facing a new, unforeseen challenge—the labor crisis. As Americans saw positive COVID-19 cases and death numbers steadily dropping during the summer months of 2021, the numbers spiked again as the new Delta variant of the virus emerged. According to an article published by Eric Rosenbam from *CNBC* on August 10, 2021, "Half of small business owners (50 percent) say it's gotten harder to find qualified people to hire compared to a year ago, according to the Q3 2021 CNBC | Momentive Small Business Survey. Almost one-third (31 percent) say they have open roles they have not been able to fill for at least three months, up from 24 percent last quarter and 16 percent in Q1 2020." In addition to this, the article also stated, "Job openings have surged to over 10 million, according to the Labor Department, the highest level on record, and it has been implied that there are over one million more jobs available than people who are searching for them." These variables have placed an enormous amount of stress and complications on business owners throughout the nation—especially small businesses.

To some extent, the repercussions of this virus have significantly and, in some ways, permanently transformed the way businesses conduct themselves in the United States. Many businesses that survived during the lockdowns are now having trouble getting people to return to work, forcing them to limit their services, hours of operation, etc. Some make the argument that the extension of the extra unemployment benefits was the motive for people not returning to work, resulting in them becoming comfortable with making more money on unemployment than they did at work, so what is the incentive to return? Others make the argument that fears of contracting the virus or the increasing demand for higher wages and more benefits resulted in people not wanting to return to work. Both arguments hold some degree of truth and significance to them. The reality is, workers have taken the competitive advantage in the balance of power between employee and employer, driven not only by the consequence of the lockdowns, but what is being portrayed in the media, what the government has done to cope, and their own personal motives.

Not only are these figures alarming, but they further support the claims as to why restaurants fail. I am not discrediting unforeseen challenges that arose from nationwide shutdowns of restaurants and played a pivotal role in the success or failure of their business during these times, but when you take time to think about why this restaurant survived and the other one didn't, what did the first do differently to ensure their survival? The "cause" or the "why" of any failure or success is deepest rooted in the entrepreneurs understanding of their values.

What do they believe in and why? How do their values affect the business decisions they make on a daily basis? The president and CEO of the National Restaurant Association, Tom Bené, said it best: "For an industry built on service and hospitality, the last six months have challenged the core understanding of our business." Those values should be instilled into the core of any restaurant owner's business. Prior to COVID-19, the restaurant already had one of the highest failure rates of all industries.

The data we now have available challenges the very foundational values of any restaurant owners' value system. Tom Bené makes another important point, stating, "Our survival for this comes down to the creativity and entrepreneurship of owners, operators, and employees. Across the board, from independent owners to multi-unit franchise operators, restaurants are losing money every month, and they continue to struggle to serve their communities and support their employees." This quote leads perfectly into the focal point of this book: The faith-based values we instilled in our business have sustained us for the last thirty-eight years and counting. Our businesses values reflect and are centered upon the Benedictine Hallmarks the Benedictine Monastic Community lives by. These values are:

- Love of Neighbor as Yourself
- Prayer: A Life Guided by Mindfulness, Faithfulness, and Deep Reflection
- Stability
- Daily Conversion
- Obedience
- Discipline
- Humility
- Stewardship
- Hospitality
- Community

What is something Tom Bené and Benedictine monks have in common? They both believe an individual in a position of leadership and service should live by some of the same values I just listed. The point being is whether you are a faith-filled person or not, if an entrepreneur or person in any leadership position centers their purpose around these core values, they will be mentally prepared to overcome any challenge they are faced with, both seen and unforeseen. In the chapters to come, I will break down the meaning of each of these values, examples of their relevance, and an application of how you, the reader, can implement these values into your business's culture.

CHAPTER 3

Love Your Neighbor as Yourself

———

"Do to others whatever you would like them to do to you. This is the essence of all that is taught in the law and the prophets."
—(MT. 7:12, NLT)

What is the meaning of the word "love"? It can be defined and interpreted several different ways. From a broad standpoint, love can be best defined as "an intense feeling of deep affection" (Dictionary.com s.v. 2021). My parents and I believe love is best expressed through actions rather than only stating it. From an early age in life, most of us are taught to "treat others the way you want to be treated." No matter our age, this can be challenging at times, and at other times, come naturally. But the older I get, the more I see the truth and value of that important lesson.

One of the most "make or break" values of a leader within any organization is this: to love your neighbor as yourself.

Treat others the way you want to be treated. This chapter will focus on the direct correlation between how business leaders define love, the religious definition of love, how the two of these two definitions have the same intentions, and how being a "servant leader" creates a work environment centered on building, sustaining, and maintaining healthy and prosperous relationships that ensure success.

From St. Benedict's perspective, to love your neighbor as yourself means, "Benedictine life, like that of all Christians, is first and foremost a response to God's astonishing love for humankind, a love expressed in the free gift of his beloved Son, Jesus Christ" (San Beda University. 2022). To St. Benedict, love is at the top of his list of tools used to accomplish good deeds and works. Arguably one of the most important teachings of Jesus, documented over two thousand years ago in scripture is, "Thou shalt love the Lord thy God with all thy heart, and with all thy soul, and with all thy mind. This is the first and great commandment. And the second is like unto it, Thou shalt love thy neighbor as thyself" (Matthew 22:37-39).

In addition to this definition, other similar interpretations can be found throughout scripture, all with the same message: Love your neighbor as yourself. This verse can be interpreted as you first and foremost love God with all your heart, his love will radiate within you, and will naturally deluge over all of your personal actions and thoughts, thus giving us the mindfulness to love others like we love God. As it was written in the first book of the Bible, Genesis 1:27, "So God created man in His own image; in the image of God He created him; male and female He created them."

It is only fitting that if we believe God created humans in the image of himself, why wouldn't we love others the way we love ourselves? Though all of mankind has its micro-level differences, we are all still the same. Well-known theologian, Ian Paul, breaks this down by stating, "They, too, are creatures of infinite worth and dignity. They, too, are frail and finite, weak and willful, selfish and stupid, deprived and depraved—just as you are. And then we treat them as we ourselves want and need to be treated: with love—which means with respect, affection, honesty, and kindness."

From a business perspective, to love your neighbor as yourself is best defined as, "A feeling of warm personal attachment or deep affection, as for a parent, child, or friend" (Dictionary. com s.v. 2021). Essentially, the job of the leader is to love the people. It is also important to define what a leader is. A leader is "a guiding or directing head, as of an army, movement, or political group" (Dictionary.com s.v. 2021). If a leader doesn't lead with love, how can they expect the people they lead to behave the same way? How can they expect them to be happy with themselves and happy to be serving in the organization or business they're part of? How can they expect the people they lead to become mirrors of this value and express it to those they serve? A good and effective leader takes the initiative to do everything they can to ensure the happiness and well-being of the people they lead.

Every business or organization comes into existence with the intention of providing a product or service that can help others. If the leader does not first lead with love and focuses more on themselves, their wealth, their job, their own feelings, and not others, the business or organization is susceptible to failure. One of the main reasons businesses or organizations fail is because training of managers or other leaders within the organization is poor or inconsistent. If leaders master the ability to truly love others as themselves, they will motivate their followers to do the best job they can, lift them up when they're down, listen to their concerns, act in accordance with their needs, mentor them when they fail, congratulate them when they're successful, and truly treat others the way they want to be treated. Don't we all want to be treated this way?

Now that we have defined the differences between these two important interpretations of loving your neighbor as yourself, it is now necessary to compare the similarities of them both, showing how they are two of the same, and why this value is the most important value to embed into the culture of your business or organization. Theoretically speaking, if you are a leader in a business or organization and have a religious background, specifically in Christianity, it may come more naturally to understand the religious definition of loving your neighbor as yourself and/or have an easier time implementing this value into your business or organization, having lived a life based upon this teaching from your religion.

If you are a leader without a religious background, you may have a different definition of what "love" means and what causes you to act with love before all else. If we draw back on the broad definition of love stated in the beginning of the chapter, that being "an intense feeling of deep affection," we can begin to correlate this definition to why an entrepreneur or leader decides to become one. Love from the perspective of a leader and the Benedictines both place a focus on loving humankind. In life, there are constant occurrences or events that draw us in and give us the desire to help those less fortunate or those in need—something as little as giving a homeless person some money or something as large as starting a nationwide non-profit like the Wounded Warrior Project.

When an individual believes they are called to make a change for the better of many, a call to leadership or entrepreneurship of a business or organization, they have a calling to provide a product of service for which there is a common need to benefit the lives of those they wish to serve. That individual has an intense feeling or deep affection for creating a solution to either a common problem, need, or desire, which in turn serves as their "why" for choosing to create their business or organization. If the entrepreneur is to be successful, they must understand that they must personally act on this intense feeling or deep affection by providing the services or products they believe are needed with the assistance of others within the business or organization whose values align with theirs.

In addition, how can the entrepreneur or leader live up to its business's or organization's "why" without having the same emotion of this kind of love for others? Specifically, the ones they desire to serve? It's all relevant. When one expresses love by their intense feeling or deep affection to serve others while providing a beneficial product or service, they are loving others as themselves by making the necessary sacrifices to create the business or organization they envisioned. You can be an entrepreneur or leader without having a religious background and still be successful with the core value of love as your "why." The other values mentioned in this book are built on this foundation. If you're able to love yourself and others, practicing and living by any of these other values becomes achievable and will sustain you in the long term.

From personal experience, my family's business is built upon this value. My father and uncle grew up in an active Roman Catholic household. Loving their neighbor as themselves was embedded into their heads at a young age. Through hard work and countless blessings, their business has provided them with the opportunity to give back to the community and other organizations, providing employment to thousands of people in the community throughout the last thirty-eight years and giving them a stable source of income and the financial freedom necessary to provide for their needs.

If any of our employees or friends were ever in a tough position in life and needed help, we have been there to help however and whenever we could. If any of our patrons had any specific requests, accommodations, or needs, we have always gone out of our way to make sure we accommodated those needs to the best of our ability. It is through our love of God and a recognition that every human being has equal value and dignity that fuels our love and our why to help others.

One of our former team members, Paulette Giesel, has dedicated twenty-nine years of her life to our business. Paulette started as a dish washer and climbed the organization's hierarchy ladder to eventually becoming the general manager. She shared with me countless memories of how the value of loving your neighbor as yourself has been the top value at Luigi's. One example she gave really stood out to me. She said, "When my husband was laid off, my cousin helped me get a job at Luigi's while she was working there. When I started working there, your father, Eddie, and Skip didn't only care about me; they cared about my family. Skip would ask, 'How is your husband doing? Give me an application; I will find him a job,' and he did." Paulette continued, "He helped my husband get his job at PennDot a year later. He always told my husband if you know of anybody else that needs a job, let me know, I will do whatever I can to help somebody. It wasn't just the restaurant or me as a worker there he cared about—he cared about my family."

Another example is told by one of our patrons, Mary Beth Campbell, who's been dining at Luigi's for over twenty years. Mary Beth and her husband, Ike, spent every single Saturday night at Luigi's. It was more than just grabbing dinner; it was the whole experience of spending quality time with one another while enjoying the conversations with many staff members, who always looked forward to seeing them. Mary Beth shared, "The word 'family' has a unique and totally infused meaning at Luigi's. New employees quickly under-stand that EACH patron is special, more than just because of material reasons, but because we CHOSE to dine there."

She then goes on to say, "During my husband's terminal illness, my family and I received numerous texts, calls, and even quick visits to our home. Many offers of help, care pack-ages, prayers and meals. Soon after his passing, our son, Brett, took me out for dinner to Luigi's. We were greeted with many hugs, gifts, and even a free meal. At the time of Ike's service, the Tate family and many of their staff drove to the funeral home to not only share in our pain but bring us encourage-ment and support. After the service, they prepared a special area for my immediate family to gather and celebrate Ike's life." Mary Beth concluded, "The wonderful truth in all of this is that it was NOT a unique occurrence just for my family! I have heard from others how the Luigi's family has been there for them as well. It is simply how they treat their patrons, as family, not just customers."

At the beginning of the pandemic and throughout its duration, we became even more conscious of placing an extra focus on sustaining the physical, practical, emotional, and spiritual needs of our staff, especially during takeout only. During this time, over a million Pennsylvanians were unemployed. Both staff we kept employed and staff we had to temporarily lay off were given relief bonuses. These bonuses came from the PPP grant we received and directly out of our pockets. We took a pay cut to ensure they had the financial means to continue to provide food, shelter, pay their bills on time, and for other necessities they needed. Having to rapidly restructure our entire business operations overnight, we included the staff in decision-making to ensure their opinions were not only heard but acted upon so they were still motivated to come to and enjoy being at work. These actions fulfilled many of their emotional needs as well.

Allowing them the opportunity to play a part in critical decision-making affecting their job performance made them more efficient while making it more meaningful. We constantly remind them how much we appreciate them and how grateful we are to have them. Loving our staff as ourselves not only retains them but inspires others to want a job at Luigi's as well. Most importantly, we give them at least one day off for rest or worship to allow them to reconnect with themselves and those important to them. We recognize how important it is to have a day to escape reality—to rest, worship, meditate, adventure, or whatever they need to do to reconnect with their inner peace and well-being.

Like I mentioned earlier, love expresses itself in action. A leader implements this value by taking time to recognize the value and worthiness of the people they lead and serve. Leaders like this are referred to as a "servant leader." A servant leader "focuses primarily on the growth and well-being of people and the communities to which they belong. While traditional leadership generally involves the accumulation and exercise of power by one at the 'top of the pyramid,' servant leadership is different. The servant leader shares power, puts the needs of others first, and helps people develop and perform as highly as possible" (Greenleaf.org 2021). First and foremost, they recognize the value and worth of every individual. A servant leader needs to be ambitious and passionate about serving others. People in leadership positions can be motivated by different things such as wealth, status, recognition, or other materialistic desires. An effective servant leader that loves others like themselves is motivated by serving others and aiding in their prosperity rather than their own self-driven desires that come with success.

This value is important both from a religious and business perspective. A servant leader leads with empathy and compassion, not envy or greed. "The most natural thing in the world is for human beings to connect and build relationships. Our entire species is wired for social interaction and for the development of friendships and affections" (Thane Bellomo, 2020). Every relationship formed should focus on providing both parties with the ability to prosper and flourish. Leadership without admiration and care will never lead to long-term prosperity for you or the people you employ or serve. It takes the collaboration of both parties in a relationship to achieve whatever their shared goal is. An effective leader shares responsibility with those they serve, shares in their team's accomplishments and failures together, and uses them both as benchmarks to be better at providing the services your business or organization provides.

Author Susan Bruno from The Transition House has provided readers with an excellent list of mental practices that, if exercised daily, can help you to better love yourself. Those five practices are:

- **Practice self-care:** "Taking care of your basic needs is essential to being mentally healthy. Exercising, maintaining proper nutrition, and getting enough sleep all help to improve and maintain good mental health. But self-care can be difficult for some. Things like brushing your teeth, taking a shower, or wearing clean clothes each day might seem simple, but they can be tough to do, especially if you struggle with something like depression, anxiety, or another form of mental illness. When you feel low or stressed, self-care can be put on the back burner, but it should be just the opposite. Practicing self-care daily, no matter how small, is a healthy habit and a great way to practice self-love" (Susan Bruno. 2021).
- **Focus on your needs, not your wants:** "While you might want to do things that feel good or exciting, practicing self-love means choosing to do the things that keep you focused on your goals and moving toward a healthier,

happier life. This can be especially true for people struggling with addiction. Practicing self-love means putting your needs—like choosing recovery and working toward sobriety—before your wants" (Susan Bruno. 2021).

- **Set healthy boundaries:** "Allow yourself to say no to things that wear you down, or that harm you physically or emotionally. This applies to your work, personal life, relationships, and recreational activities. Surround yourself with a healthy support system that includes people who respect your boundaries and who will keep you accountable. Protecting yourself from people who don't wish you well is essential to self-love" (Susan Bruno. 2021).

- **Forgive others:** "Practicing forgiveness can take time, especially if you don't feel ready to let go of past hurts. Counseling can help you learn how to forgive and can teach you the coping skills you need to let go of trauma or hurt from your past. Practicing forgiveness can facilitate healing and ultimately allow you to develop a sense of self-love" (Susan Bruno. 2021.).

- **Forgive yourself:** "Just like practicing self-care, forgiving ourselves can take a back seat when we feel low or stressed. We might forget that we need to forgive ourselves just as much as we need to forgive others. Remember, in life, no one is perfect and it's normal to make mistakes when we are growing or learning. That is just a part of being human. Forgiving yourself can be difficult but not impossible, and it is something that you can learn to do through counseling" (Susan Bruno. 2021).

Loving others is dependent on your ability to love yourself. If you cannot truly love yourself, you cannot truly love others. As a leader, it is detrimental to your long-term success that you love yourself and love others as yourself. If you only focus on the needs of the product and not the needs of your people, your odds of failing dramatically increase. To further back that claim, psychologist Dr. Darren J. Edwards says, "Developing a healthy relationship with yourself may be the key to developing a healthy relationship with another. Studies have demonstrated that people who are more self-compassionate have more positive and higher-quality relationships than those who do not. Perhaps, therefore, the most important relationship you have really is with yourself."

Living with this mindset better prepares all individuals to handle adversity, hardships, or failures with a positive outlook—an attitude that through failure, comes success. Prioritize building, sustaining, and maintaining loyalty, trust, and care between yourself, your staff, and the people you serve. Remind your staff and those you serve frequently that you appreciate them through verbal communications, actions, and rewards. Allow them to take time off to reconnect with their inner peace. Place an equal importance on their personal needs, the business's needs, and your own. You cannot have a healthy and successful business or organization without addressing the personal needs of those you work with. Be the leader who would make your God, your parents, or your loved ones happy. Most importantly, use your leadership position to advance the health and well-being of those you work with and serve.

Make the initiative of getting to personally know the people you serve. Make an effort to know their name, show them you care about them and their family, and address their needs and concerns. These lessons are taught to us both through scripture and literature on good leadership practices. Whether you currently abide by this value or not, taking time for prayer, meditation, or liturgy allows a leader the opportunity to reflect on this value, and how they can be better at it, which leads me into the next value.

CHAPTER 4

Prayer: A Life Guided by Mindfulness, Faithfulness, and Deep Reflection

------

"Ask and it will be given to you; seek and you will find; knock and the door will be opened to you."

—MATTHEW 7:7

Ask, and it will be given to you. Seek, and you will find. Knock, and the door will be opened to you. Now repeat that a few times out loud. Ponder those words. What do they mean to you? Have there been specific times in your life when there was something you yearned to have and couldn't help but to ask aloud for help? Have you ever wanted something so badly that you sought it out until you accomplished it? Have you ever been so persistent in your desire to acquire something that you continued to seek it until you eventually acquired it? If so, these actions were most likely subconsciously rooted in either your personal mindfulness, faithfulness, or deep reflection.

Before we dive into the significance of this value, let us start by defining the words prayer, mindfulness, faithfulness, and reflection.

Merriam-Webster's online encyclopedia provides us with two different yet similar definitions of prayer:

Prayer (religious definition): an address (such as a petition) to God or a god in word or thought.

Example: Dear God, I pray that you continue to keep my co-workers protected from evil, illness, or harm, especially throughout the COVID-19 pandemic.

Prayer (non-religious definition): an earnest request or wish.

Example: It is our prayer that we find a cure for cancer.

It is evident that both definitions claim prayer to be placing hope in a greater being or power to help you overcome a problem or achieve something you're longing for. One places their hope in God, while the other places their hope in some sort of divine intervention from a greater being or force. When we're mindful of the present moment, of our current surroundings or situations, or of our interactions with others, our prayers become more natural and meaningful. In our prayers, we either pray for things we want or need or we give thanks. From our prayers comes faithfulness to the things we pray about and for. When we remain faithful to our daily tasks, responsibilities, or goals, we must allow time for reflection. It is through reflection we become conscious of what we are doing well, what we can improve on, what we need to do to achieve whatever it is we set out to accomplish, and what we can do to be a better person. What does mindfulness, faithfulness, and reflection mean? According to Dictionary.com, these three words are best defined as:

Mindfulness: a technique in which one focuses one's full attention only on the present, experiencing thoughts, feelings, and sensations but not judging them.

Example: A leader mindful of their surroundings, particularly their struggles, can better manage stress and composure.

Faithfulness: the fact or quality of being true to one's word or commitments, as to what one has pledged to do, professes to believe, etc.

Example: A leader who commits themselves to the preservation of the well-being of their team will result in their team's faithfulness to the organization they belong to.

Reflection: a thought occurring in consideration or meditation.

Example: I will take time to reflect on my failures, discover what went wrong, and what I can do differently next time to be successful.

Now having defined these terms, let us reflect on their significance to leadership. Prayer, to some extent, can be inter-related to optimism (hopefulness and confidence about the future or the successful outcome of something.) A successful business leader remains optimistic in their beliefs—a belief they themselves, their staff, and their patrons are all destined to something good happening to them in their life. Sure, life presents us with many hardships, some foreseen and some unforeseen. It is important for a leader not to dwell on the things that went wrong or didn't go as planned. Rather, accept the circumstances life has presented you with and remain optimistic that something good will come out of the bad experience. Even if it's just a learning lesson.

If everything went our way in life all the time, life would be boring. There would be nothing to live for. It is through the hardship that life gives us the ultimate opportunity for growth. Life has a constant roller coaster style to it. We are presented with many highs and many lows. It is through the adversity we face at our lows that make the highs so much more meaningful. The main value that gets business leaders through the lows and hard times is a steadfast mind, focus on prayer, and earnest hope or wish we give to God or a greater being or force; a hope in them that they will get us through whatever hardship we face.

Directly correlated with that is mindfulness. Leaders with a religious background often exercise this value through their prayer and make time to be either by themselves or with others praying by their side. In their prayer, they are conscious of who they are and what they are doing while praying for guidance and direction toward the person they aspire to be. "Benedictine leaders welcome the mindfulness of the gifted nature of creation regardless of one's belief traditions. (Compendium, p. 23) That being said, a Benedictine worldview sees a leader of any faith or 'non-faith' tradition that is not faithful to a disciplined and mindful practice of daily reflection as impoverished" (Hisker, W. J. & Urick, M. J. 2019). Both leaders with faith and those without are strengthened by the daily practice of mindfulness.

Practicing mindfulness is equally important for leaders without a religious background, nor is it necessary for an effective leader to have a religious background to practice mindfulness. A study conducted by Marissa Levin from Harvard University in 2018 discovered "when leaders are stressed, their anxiety can be felt across the entire organization, often to the point where good employees will walk away from a job to save their own health." In addition, Marissa's study revealed "when leaders fail to manage their stress in a constructive way, more than 50 percent of their employees perceive their leader as harmful or ineffective. Further when leaders are unable to manage stress, employees lose their drive to advance within the company." This further proves their point that practicing mindfulness serves as one of the most effective ways to manage stress. They go on to state that when a leader exercises mindfulness, they increase the hope, optimism, self-efficacy, and resilience of themselves and those they lead and serve. Mindfulness encompasses all four of these character traits, proven to be crucial to the success and longevity of any business or organization.

According to Marissa's research, "The first step to becoming a mindful leader is to develop self-awareness. We cannot change what we don't know. Leaders can raise their own mindfulness by paying attention to how they are engaging with people and within situations at work." They too, like our definition of mindfulness, stress the importance of having self-awareness of our words and how we communicate with others; our actions and how we interact with others. Once we become aware of those behaviors, we can then begin to focus on how we can improve our awareness of the needs and concerns of those whom we lead and serve. We become more conscious of how our actions and our communication affect those around us and how we can be more of a servant leader to those whose lives we are a part of.

Faithfulness goes hand-in-hand with mindfulness. "Now, a person who is put in charge as a manager must be faithful." 1 Corinthians 4:2-4. A leader with a religious background is first and foremost committing to living a life according to their religious beliefs and behaving in a manner that parallels the guidelines established in scripture, given to us from God. They believe God is the guiding or model figure helping us shape our actions in a way intended to serve him and his people—that being all of humankind. Faithfulness from a non-religious definition basically has the same definition as defined earlier in the chapter: the commitment to sticking to your word and standing by your team members' side through the good times and especially the bad. Never betray your commitment to them and the mission you and your team collectively are a part of. Faithfulness is parallel to loyalty. A leader who is successful long-term has faithfulness and loyalty to their business or organization, the people they lead, and the people they serve. Ensure everyone within your organization mirrors the values of the business, they continue to play their role within the organization, and their vision is aligned with yours.

One of our head chefs, Vickie, often discusses her faith with my father and said, "Without my faith, I would not have made it to where I am today. I believe we are all God's children, and we are meant to try our best to help others and not judge." She goes on to say, "Lou is pretty good at being mindful of the employees' needs, wants, and concerns both inside and outside of the workplace. Not only is he faithful to his religion, but faithful to his team. He has always followed through with his promises and was there for me if I ever needed anything, or felt I needed to address something." Reflection is another value both Vickie and my father share. She mentioned to me, "Almost every time I come home after work, I replay things that happened at work in my mind and thought I should've done this instead or next time this happens I am going to respond differently. It is through reflection where I learn the most."

Another one of our main chefs, Jeff McQuisten, who has been dedicated to our business for over eighteen years, does not have a religious background, but shares this value with us. Jeff told me, "I've never been the type to pray to God. I don't even know what it's like. I was never raised to pray to God, so I never truly understood it or tried it. I have always been hopeful and optimistic though. Good or bad, I have always remained hopeful and optimistic in my wishes. I know you and your dad pray to God all of the time. I know you guys pray for me and for others. Whether you pray to God or just pray in the form of an earnest hope or wish, that it is a good value to have, and the fruits of your prayers show in your actions and your speech.

When your dad gives me pep talks, whether it is a good or a bad day, it always ends well with a handshake and a hug. He might bring up an issue, or I might bring one to his attention, and there is always a teaching moment. He has taught me a lot on how to be mindful of others or current situations, and how to control how I feel and react, as well as taking time to reflect on those feelings or actions." He concluded, "I have always been faithful to this business and to my job. I am passionate about what I do and providing the customer food that exceeds their expectations. Your dad has always been there for me, and I will always be there for you guys, the staff, customers, and the business."

Human beings have a natural tendency to be reactionary, especially to something new or strange. The one thing humans have that all other life on Earth does not is the gift of free will: the ability to think before you react, be mindful of your speech and actions, reflect on them, the ability to pray for what you need, and the faithfulness to stay committed to your prayers, helping you achieve whatever it is you need in life. My father has told me on several occasions that "not only do you have to be mindful of others' wants, needs, and concerns, but you have to be mindful of how you respond to those things, putting yourself in their position, and try to find a solution that best benefits both parties." A critical part of leadership is accepting you are not perfect and need guidance and help. You pray for the things you need, good and bad. You remain mindful of your prayers in your thoughts, speech, and actions, then reflect on the good and the bad.

Your reflection of self opens your mind to what you're doing well, what you can do better, and how you can be better.

Human beings were created to work together and use each other's strengths to complement each other's weaknesses. You do not want to be a leader of an organization with team members only there for a paycheck or for status. You want to build a team just as faithful to you, the organization, and the people the organization serves, as you are to them. In a world of instant gratification and entitlement, it may seem more natural for people to leave a business or organization where the company's values no longer align with their values. In a world of envy and greed, a leader must remain centered on not placing 100 percent of their focus on their own personal wealth and success. Rather, they prioritize the success and well-being of those they lead equally as their own. Success and failure start with top leadership. It is important now more than ever to stay committed to those you lead and those you serve, listening to them, hearing them, and acting in a way that best serves them.

Through mindfulness and faithfulness comes reflection. Leadership author Palena Neale states, "Self-reflection in leadership means carving out time to review yourself as a leader and is critical for your leadership development. It involves examining your current level of skills, your strengths, weaknesses, behavioral patterns, and how you seek to influence others. It is also about interrogating your values, goals and ambitions." This action of self-reflection can be done through a variety of different ways. Each and every person has their own special way of doing things. Self-reflection can be exercised through prayer, meditation, physical exercise, talking to yourself or others you trust and seek advice from, reading, etc. Self-reflection can stem from any activity that helps you release your inner peace.

Dedicating time to this practice is a viable function of leadership. Without taking time to recognize your own strengths and weaknesses, how you can improve, recognize who you are, who you want to be, where you are, and where you want to be? How can you lead others in an appropriate manner correlating with the needs and purpose of the business or organization you oversee? Taking time to self-reflect better equips you as a leader to inspire and encourage others to act in the same way, thus giving them the opportunity to grow through reflection as well. As Boniface Wimmer famously said, "Forward, always forward, everywhere forward." It is in the present that we take time to reflect on the past with intentions of better preparing for the future. This can be done through self-reflection.

In our own business, my family and I have a religious background we actively practice and live by. Making time for daily prayer leads into mindfulness, faithfulness, and self-reflection. Our prayers come from our mindful examination of our personal needs, the needs of our business, staff, and patrons. Amid that mindfulness, we further commit ourselves to being faithful to those needs. In the act of faithfully addressing those needs, we take time to reflect on the approach we took in addressing those needs. This reflection then leads to prayer. Living by this daily spiritual cycle frees our mind of every day distractions. It allows us to not get caught up on things we cannot control. Rather, it allows us to accept things the way they are while praying or hoping for the ability to make changes we desire to make.

It is through these times we grow to accept our failures and shortcomings, using them as a learning lesson to help us become the best leaders we can be. In my opinion, mindfulness is the most important. Without mindfulness, we question what we're faithful to, we have less of a reason for making time for reflection, and our prayers become more self-centered. Being mindful of our thoughts, speech, and actions give us more meaningful and practical prayers. From those prayers comes the ability to help us stay faithful to those we serve, ultimately giving us something more meaningful to reflect on.

I'll give you an example of how I believe my prayers are answered. When I pray for strength, God presents me with challenges requiring me to be strong. When I pray for patience, God presents me with situations where I need to be patient. When I pray for good health, God presents me with opportunities to improve it. It is easy to pray to God or place an earnest hope or trust in something. What can be difficult is being open to the signs we are given in life that directly correlate with our prayers. When I pray for patience, I can't expect to magically wake up one day and have an unprecedented level of patience. I must understand patience, or anything else I pray for, requires time and constant effort, and most importantly, an open mind. Having a mind open to whatever life gives us allows us to make the most of the present moment and better recognize an opportunity to grow or the answer to our prayers.

We encourage staff regularly to take time to do things that bring them peace on their days off. We routinely give each department of the business a brief pep talk where we talk about the issues at hand, give them the opportunity to raise their own concerns, and contribute to the resolve of the problem, all while encouraging them to reflect on these problems and focus on how we can all become better at the services we provide. It is through moments like this, where we personally involve them in decision making, and encourage them to think with a forward and optimistic mindset, where we all get the desired results in due time. My family and I regularly pray for the peace, happiness, and overall well-being of our staff and patrons. We make it known to them we also have our shortcomings and things we could do better, reminding everyone that if we take the time to continue to pray, be mindful of our actions, stay faithful to our services, and reflect on who we are and who we want to be, we can achieve great things.

Social worker and author Dr. Carla Naumburg provided six mental practices a leader (or anyone) can exercise daily to become more mindful.

- **Start When It's Easy:** "Many people get interested in mindfulness as a way to deal with stress or difficult situations, and this is a great idea. However, trying to be mindful for the first time in the middle of a crisis is a lot like trying to score the game-winning goal when you've never gone to a single practice. Don't make it harder for yourself! Start with the pleasant moments, and you'll be ready to deal with life's challenges when they come your way" (Carla Naumburg. 2018).

- **Pay Attention to Something You Do Every Day:** "A great way to start is to pick one or two activities you do every day—such as brushing your teeth, riding the bus to work, or reading a book to your children at bedtime—and get in the habit of paying attention to what you're doing. Your mind will wander, possibly within a few seconds, but don't sweat it. Just bring your attention back to your teeth or the book" (Carla Naumburg. 2018).

- **Approach Situations with Curiosity:** "If you're not sure how to respond to a situation, or if you're feeling frustrated in ways that aren't helpful, try getting curious about what is happening instead. You can't be angry and interested at the same time. It just doesn't work that way. Not only will your curiosity help you get out of a difficult headspace, but it will likely help you gain a little more clarity so you can make the most informed choice about how to move forward" (Carla Naumburg. 2018).

- **Remember the Four Ts:** "Those stand for: transitions, teatime, toilet, and telephone. I've expanded on this idea from Meena Srinivasan, author of *Teach, Breathe, Learn: Mindfulness In and Out of the Classroom*. Each time you are moving from one activity to the next, drinking tea or coffee, using the bathroom, or checking your phone, take a couple deep breaths and come back to the present moment" (Carla Naumburg. 2018).

- **Breathe Whenever You Can:** "Breathing is a key mindfulness practice because it is something we always do out of necessity, and it's also a good way to bring our awareness back to the here and now. Taking three or four deep breaths (and paying attention to them) at any given moment can help you calm down and focus" (Carla Naumburg. 2018).

- **Ground Yourself Physically:** "If concentrating on your breathing isn't quite enough, sit down and notice how the chair feels under your body. Put your hands flat on the counter or a table, and notice how the hard, cool surface feels. Keep a small stone handy and run your fingers across it. These and similar actions will bring your awareness into the present" (Carla Naumburg. 2018).

CHAPTER 5

Stability

"Traditions are our roots and a profile of who we are as individuals and who we are as a family. They are our roots, which give us stability and a sense of belonging—they ground us."

—LINDA BASTIANICH

When searching for a job, either directly out of high school or college, or throughout their entire working life before retirement, people commonly have a natural desire to find a job that brings meaning to their life and fulfills their financial needs, emotional needs, physical needs, spiritual needs, or all the above. Each of these needs and their fulfillment are important factors that bring value and meaning to the employee, employer, and the workplace. On average, when someone finds that opportunity, the work they engage in aligns with their personal values. Finding work that aligns with your values gives your work meaning results not just in job satisfaction, but more importantly, stability within the workplace.

Whether it be the employee or the employer, it is human nature to seek stability within your workplace. What exactly is stability? According to Dictionary.com, stability is defined as "steadfastness; constancy, as of character or purpose." When one finds stability in their workplace, they find meaning in their work. Stability results in loyalty, loyalty results in trust, and trust results in the continuous commitment and long-term success of the business or organization.

More often than not, we hear about leaders who focus more on the short-term gains of fame and fortune rather the long-term needs of their team and the people they're in business to serve, ultimately resulting in the business's or organization's demise within a short period of time. Why? People don't want to work for someone who prioritizes their own needs over the needs of others. Leaders who treat their employees as "resources" for their own benefit, rather than suspending their own needs or desires to ensure the well-being of those they lead and serve has never resulted in long-term success and stability.

The short-lived success and ultimate failure of the biotech company, Theranos, is a perfect example of a company that cared more about their own self-interests rather than the needs of their employees and customers. Theranos was founded in 2004 by a Stanford dropout named Elizabeth Holmes who sought to revolutionize not just blood testing, but healthcare with machines for consumers that spared the pain of traditional venal blood draws and tested for a battery of potential ailments using just a few drops of blood (Mary Juetten. 2018).

Holmes, a young, witty, and well-spoken businesswoman under the age of thirty, quickly rose to fame throughout Silicon Valley and the entire nation. This popularity was fueled by the attention she received by several media outlets and other high-profile individuals in the nation. She became so narrowly focused on her own successes that she became blind to the needs of her team. In 2015, eleven years later, the demise of Theranos came quickly after it was exposed that the blood-testing machines they created largely didn't work and the company had been both faking proficiency testing and using other commercial machines to complete the tests it claimed were being done on its machines (Forbes, 2018). Theranos officially ceased their operations in 2018.

After these revelations, it was soon discovered Holmes had created an organizational structure that didn't hold her and other key members accountable for personal and corporate ethics. While Holmes gained the support from the media, she lost the stability of her business. Rather than accepting and listening to the concerns of her top employees and other key stakeholders in the company on how they can correct these issues and provide a better product, she fired everyone who challenged her and blamed them for the failures the company experienced rather than placing the blame on herself. These actions resulted in the failure of her business.

In the web article "Benedictine Way of Life," Stella Maris College states that St. Benedict's definition of stability is "the vow of stability proclaims rootedness, 'at-homeness,' that this place and this monastic family will endure...Benedict believed, as we do, that the true wisdom necessary for leadership can only be achieved through a long-term commitment to engaging others that goes beyond achieving private short-term gain" (Hisker, W. J. & Urick, M. J. 2019). The message St. Benedict wants us to understand is that stability shapes the entire community. Stability within an organization is created when members share and live by the same values, resulting in the members within that community feeling at home, thus ensuring their commitment to the health, well-being, and longevity of the business or organization in which they serve.

Within the Benedictine community, there are rules and guidelines members within that community must agree to live by. Those rules can be found in the book *The Rule of St. Benedict*, which are built upon many values and all of which each member must also agree with and live by. It is human nature to give way to earthly desires or motives but restraining yourself from giving into those desires for the overall well-being of those in your community result in stability within the organization. "Thus, Benedictine leadership is evidenced through a long-term commitment to community and the common good" (Hisker, W. J. & Urick, M. J. 2019). To summarize the two definitions, long-term stability places an emphasis on preserving your human assets and operational assets equally.

Our bar manager, Marilyn Haslego, has been a loyal team member of Luigi's for over twenty-three years. Marilyn is a testament to the stability of the business. When asked about how she has received stability at Luigi's for over two decades, she answered, "I LOVE my job as bar manager! It seriously doesn't feel like work most of the time, especially when we're busy! I know if I need time off for whatever reason, especially if it was family related, Louie is always accommodating. He understands that family comes first." She goes on to say, "Our employer is very loyal to his employees. He goes above and beyond to let us know how much he appreciates what we do for the business. If I propose a change to something, he listens, and we work together on creating a solution. This is the first time I have worked for an employer whom I haven't had to ask for a pay raise. He sees your value and rewards you accordingly."

Like the Benedictine community, the business world seeks stability within their organizations. Stability within the business's or organization's culture is defined as "predictable, rule-oriented, and bureaucratic. These organizations aim to coordinate and align individual effort for greatest levels of efficiency. When the environment is stable and certain, these cultures may help the organization be effective by providing stable and constant levels of output" (Github Inc. 2021). Through years of research and development, businesses adopting Operational Excellence methodologies and the tools associated with it have proven to increase performance, mitigate or eliminate forms of waste, and enhance employee empowerment, resulting in making the operations of the organization more efficient.

"Drawing from continuous improvement and other tools, companies pursuing operational excellence adopt a mindset of problem solving, teamwork, and top-line growth, allowing them to create more value for customers" (smartsheet, 2019.). These kinds of methodologies not only create more value to the customer but create a deeper sense of value and stability to the people performing those tasks within their organization. When your staff feels empowered and valued, they become more passionate about finding new ways to become more efficient at their job, they're committed to understanding the tasks at hand, and feel confident in taking the initiative to help find solutions to problems within their job responsibilities, and within the organization. Implementing continuous improvement tools such as the ones listed below can result in developing a more valuable and stable work culture.

- **Developing Standard Operating Processes:** Visual diagrams or illustrations describing step-by-step actions of how a particular job or process should be executed, thus creating a standard of the expectations of the actions and results of that particular job or process. Having this standard operating process creates consistency in the output of that process, as well as consistency in training, so anyone can be trained to execute the process the same way as the person before them. Improving a process won't be effective until the people performing the job contribute to the design of the standard operating process and execute accordingly.
- **Value Stream Mapping:** Mapping out the step-by-step operations of a process begins with the standard operating process and visuals of every step of the process. Key staff members and leadership use this to identify waste and value within the process. After identifying value, we know what we are doing well in the process; after identifying waste, it allows the opportunity for improvement, making it more efficient and stable.
- **Visual Work Instructions:** Similar to standard operating processes, visual work instructions serve as a training guide for new and or experienced staff members. These

instructions define the standardized step-by-step process to perform and execute a specific job or action, limiting confusion and mistakes. These instructions also can be in text, images, or both.

- **A Focus on Eliminating the Seven Common Forms of Waste within an Organization—Known by the Acronym TIMWOOD:** According to Nawras Skhmot, each letter of TIMWOOD represents the first letter of each of the seven forms of waste:
  - **Transportation**: wasted time, resources, and costs when unnecessarily moving products and materials.
  - **Inventory**: wastes resulting from excess products and material not processed.
  - **Motion**: wasted time and effort related to unnecessary movements by people.
  - **Waiting**: waste from time spent waiting for the next process step to occur.
  - **Over-Production**: waste from making more product than customer demand.
  - **Over-Processing**: waste related to more work or higher quality than required.
  - **Defects**: waste from a product or service failure to meet customer expectations.
- **Studying Process Statistics and Analyses:** Statistical analysis answers the question, "What happened?" This analysis covers data collection, analysis, modeling, interpretation, and presentation using dashboards. The statistical analysis breaks down into two sub-categories (simplilearn, 2021):
  - **Descriptive**: Descriptive analysis works with either complete or selections of summarized numerical

data. It illustrates means and deviations in continuous data and percentages and frequencies in categorical data.

- **Inferential**: Inferential analysis works with samples derived from complete data. An analyst can arrive at different conclusions from the same comprehensive data set just by choosing different samplings.

Each of these tools have proven to be vital in maintaining stability within an organization. This idea is so important to the tenets of operational excellence that the Institute for Operational Excellence defines operational excellence as "the point at which each and every employee can see the flow of value to the customer and can fix that flow before it breaks down" (smartsheet. 2019). After breaking the two definitions of stability down, we see they are both related by orienting their focus on creating an environment that can survive long-term, driven by members within that organization that share the same goals, motives, and values. This is achieved by humbling yourself to forget about your own short-term personal desires, prioritizing actions resulting in the greater good of your team and community in which you serve by including the collective thoughts, ideas, and actions of the individuals within your organization.

A leader of any business or organization can achieve a stable work culture by, first and foremost, doing as St. Benedict preaches: creating a community unified in their values, goals, and purpose. Understanding that we are meant to serve and help others, for the greater good of all, is one of the most important lessons in leadership. Once that community is created, they must put into action their values. If you claim to live by certain values but don't act on those values, are they your true virtues? When applicable, the operational excellence actions and tools listed above have been proven to result in ensuring a stable work environment.

In my family's business, we strive to create a work environment where our staff feel important, empowered, and appreciated. Through proper vetting during the interview process, we attract and hire staff that best align with our values and have the same purpose for coming to work and providing the services they do. We clearly define our values and why we are in business, what is keeping us in business, and what the customer expects and wants from us. **Our staff aren't just employees to us; they're family.** We greet them by name with a smile and acknowledge their dignity and existence. This simple gesture has proven to have a ripple effect, resulting in them also greeting each other and the people they serve with the same appeal. A few specific examples of our actions include the following:

- We make it known to them through word and deed that if they or their family ever need anything, we are there to support them. This action continually results in a deeper sense of their loyalty to the business, as well as a sense of appreciation, comfort, and stability working for us.
- We provide them with a pay rate as high as the business can possibly allow with the addition of some benefits, incentives, and bonuses. This action keeps them incentivized, knowing they have a stable income and the opportunity to make more through hard work and commitment.
- We allow for the opportunity of promotion to higher positions from within. We choose this option before hiring

someone from the outside who doesn't know the business's operations as well as our current staff does. This also gives the staff, especially those who strive to climb the chain of command, a greater sense of appreciation. Their experience is valuable, and they have the opportunity to become a leader within their department and the entire business.

• As a team, we have implemented and utilized the Operation Excellence tools listed above.

One of our main chefs, Shawn Arford, agrees that organization-wide communication is vital to long-term stability in the business. Shawn played a significant part in operational changes within the kitchen, especially during the COVID-19 pandemic. Shawn shared, "I know if I have any issue, concern, or idea about anything, my voice will be heard and respected due to the great relationship between staff and management. Something like taking catering orders where we have multiple orders in a day and discussing menus to try and keep them similar to optimize the efficiency and productivity. During the holidays, it can get very overwhelming with catering orders, but the communication, planning, and optimism by management aids in making sure we have all the resources available that are needed. Proper communication and teamwork definitely ease the mind and keep the workplace stable."

Shawn continued, "Stability can be a balance between standardization and change. Whether the change comes dramatically and unforeseen like the COVID-19 pandemic or something less dramatic like when a customer requests a meal we haven't had in a while for a weekend special, we either try to make it right then and there or, if we can't, we try to incorporate that suggestion when deciding on our weekend specials menu." He concluded, "The resilience and ability to adapt, learn, and grow from those experiences are what help keep things stable. The pandemic created new obstacles for everyone, and it was the stability we created here that gave everyone hope and the ability to persevere toward our goals while finding the best methods to reach them. Just knowing that no matter what obstacles come at us we will stay optimistic and accomplish all our goals is what makes the workplace so stable."

Working with key staff members in each department of the restaurant, we created value stream maps identifying every step of every current process within their department. From there, they help us identify areas within each process that we are doing well and areas we can improve upon that result in one of the seven forms of waste listed above. These key staff members are the ones living their job day in and day out. They have their special area of focus within their department that allows them the ability to recognize in greater detail the areas in which we are excelling and the areas creating problems, disruptions, or waste.

My father and I, as the owner/operators, oversee all operations of the business simultaneously, making it more difficult for us to identify the minute details of how our staff performs their job. It only makes sense we include them in these important operational changes. Making them a part of these changes gives them a sense of empowerment and appreciation that their boss/leader not only allows them the opportunity to voice their opinion on how they can perform their job better, but the ability to turn their opinions into actions by implementing operational changes that make their job easier for them and anyone tasked to the same job. This leadership action results in a more efficient and effective business fueled by employee innovation and optimism, better equipping us to meet the needs of the customer.

Gerry Thomchick and his wife, Debbie, have been patrons of Luigi's since the first few months of the business's life. They have seen many changes throughout the years, both physical and operational, and those changes have proven to strengthen the stability of the business. One aspect of the business that has never changed throughout these thirty-eight-plus years has been the "family feel" and "home away from home" atmosphere they've had and continue to receive from the entire Luigi's family every time they visit. Gerry shared, "Every time we have dined at Luigi's, both since its first year of existence till this day, we are treated like family by everyone who works there. From the moment you walk through the door you are greeted with a smile and more than just your server stops to say hello and check in on you. You can tell Louie and the people he has working there truly love working there." He continued, "During takeout only, I appreciated that even though they downsized the menu, there was still a nice variety and something different every week. They listened to the customers' suggestions and based some of their menu for the week on them."

Another customer previously mentioned, Scott Bassaro, said, "Since our first visit thirty-eight years ago, my family and I have always chosen Luigi's to host any of our family events: birthdays, graduations, religious celebrations, etc. When we are here, we are treated like family. Seeing the pictures on the walls and having meaningful conversations with Louie and the staff really give us a feeling that we are truly welcome here like family. We all witness him give the same treatment to other patrons, and it is truly something you rarely see anymore. We consider Luigi's our home away from home." He added, "Since I have been dining here, Louie and his staff have always been open to new ideas or suggestions from the customers. I noticed the operational changes they had made once the COVID-19 restrictions were in effect, and how they would ask their patrons for their feedback and if there is anything else they could do or change to better serve the community."

After each operational change is made, a standardized operating process is constructed to clearly list each step of how that process should be executed. These standardized operating processes serve as effective and consistent training guidelines for new employees, as well as refreshers for current employees on how to best perform the tasks associated with the job they are assigned to. These standard operating processes are permanent until there is another opportunity to make changes that make their job even more efficient. Utilizing standard operating processes absolutely ensures stability within the organization, but only short-term stability.

Why? Because life goes on, new challenges both foreseen and unforeseen arise, technology evolves, and demographics, tastes, interests, and demands change. The mentality of seeking continuous improvement of your operations within your business or organization is the only way to remain stable in the long term. You and your team must grow and adapt to changes or challenges that constantly arise.

Life is constantly evolving, resulting in the revolutionizing of how businesses and organizations operate. The effects of COVID-19 are a perfect example of how, overnight, things can drastically change the way your business or organization operates. In less than twenty-four hours, my father, our key staff members, and I had to construct brand-new standardized operating processes to adapt to takeout only and the other new restrictions on how businesses and organizations could operate during the first spike of the COVID-19 virus. In addition to making the operational changes, we utilized the statistics generated by our point-of-sale system to help us become efficient and effectively serve our customers. Those statistics included:

- **Quantity of Sales per Menu Item**: helped us decide what food items made it on our downsized temporary take-out only menu.
- **Days of Week/Time of Day**: helped us better understand what times were our busiest and slowest so we could be adequately staffed to effectively meet the customers' needs on a timely basis.
- **Order Volume**: helped us understand how many orders to expect each day, allowing us the opportunity to prepare our inventory more efficiently for the day/week and further mitigate the creation of waste.

Using these statistics, along with the input of our staff in creating new standardized operational process changes, best prepared us for the sudden changes. Even then, we still must remain open and willing to learn from our successes and our failures, continuing to push forward in our ambitions to be as operationally efficient and effective as possible. A motivated and empowered leader understands the significance of this and encourages their team to accept and adapt to change while making the necessary changes to their operating processes to ensure long-term stability—all with the same goal in mind to remain stable within our workplace by providing a steady and consistent product to our customers.

When our products and services are viewed as valuable by our customer base, their patronage and support fuels the stability of the business. To sum things up, steadiness within the workplace's culture is created when the whole team's, vision, mission, and actions are aligned, creating standardized systems of operation, and ultimately the ability to enhance those systems by adapting to changes. A leader can develop stability within their business or organization by:

- Creating an environment or culture within their organization based on a strong value system, embodied by people who share the same values, and an environment where your human assets and your operational assets are equally important to the stability of the business. A place where the people you lead and the people they serve feel at home, comfortable, and loyal to that business or organization; an environment where you, as the leader, seek the long-term commitment to the well-being of the people you lead and the community you serve, rather than using them to achieve your own short-term materialistic desires.
- Making the people you lead feel involved and appreciated. Allowing them the opportunity to raise their opinions on

how they can make themselves more efficient at their job, and letting them put that opinion into action, making the overall business or organization effective and efficient at serving the community they serve.

- Utilizing tools, applications, or technology best geared toward your specific business or organization with your team with the purpose of seeking the continuous improvement of your businesses or organizations operational processes; understanding you need to attract and retain the right people for the job that best fits their skill sets and allowing those key people in those departments to help you develop a standardized system of operations, but have the willingness to make changes to it if necessary. These actions create the foundation for long-term stability.

CHAPTER 6

Daily Conversion

___

"When you see a good person, think of becoming like her/him. When you see someone not so good, reflect on your own weak points."

—CONFUCIUS

At some point in your life, I'm sure there have been times you noticed yourself or a co-worker, friend, or relative, talk about the way someone looks, the way someone lives their life, does something you don't agree with, or even overthink about how someone talks, acts, or feels toward them. Whether these actions happen subconsciously or consciously, they are all signs of judgment. It is human nature to compare ourselves to others, but just because it is human nature, does it make it acceptable? That depends.

"Judging others has good and bad sides. When you make choices based on observing and evaluating other people, you are using an important skill. When you judge people from a negative perspective, you are doing it to make yourself feel better and as a result the judgment is likely to be harmful to both of you" (Life Coach Directory. 2019). Judgment is a character trait we all have. Judgment, like anything else in life, has its pros and cons. You make judgments every day on what to wear, when to eat, what you are going to spend your time doing, etc. This necessary ability has allowed us the opportunity to decide between right and wrong from very early on in our lives.

As we age, we become more aware of what is good and what is bad based upon our experiences—ultimately dictating the decisions we make. Contrary to this, judgment can have negative effects. If you base your conclusions on the negative qualities of yourself or another, it can result in negative feelings, reactions, or consequences for you and others. If you focus on someone's strong points and negatively compare them to your weak ones, you have already limited yourself and your ability. Rather, if you focus on someone's strong points and positively compare them to your weak points, it will result as a source of motivation to be better, to strengthen your weak points, and continue to grow.

If you are in a leadership position, critical thinking and analysis become detrimental to the type of leader you are and can make or break the leader you aspire to be. Your judgments as a leader, both good and bad, affect those whom you lead and serve, making it ever more important to rationally think about the pros and cons of any judgment before making a decision on what you say or how you act. As a leader, we are called to strengthen the weak points of those we lead through mentorship, as well as praise them on their strong points or when they are successful. This role emphasizes the importance of daily reflection and conversion.

What is daily conversion? When discussing conversion, St. Benedict uses the Latin word *conversatio*, which he defines as "the process of letting go in day-to-day life of self-centered preoccupations and false securities so that the divine life at the core of one's being becomes manifest in a trustworthy pattern of living...this transformation proceeds according to small steps; and it is tested in unexpected ways over a lifetime. To come to fruition conversatio requires stability, discipline, faithfulness and resilience" (San Beda University, 2022). St. Benedict calls upon leaders to allow themselves to become open to the process of reflection and openness to transformation; to take time to pray and reflect on our thoughts and actions, admit our wrong doings and flaws, and focus on becoming better servants of Christ so we may treat others the way he expects us to. He is calling us to be more aware of our judgments and to learn from them so we may better serve the community's needs. He wants us to learn from our mistakes daily and focus on being the best servant leaders we can be.

A long-time family friend and patron since our origins, Dennis Previte, beautifully elaborated on what daily conversion is and how it has lived at Luigi's. "People have many different kinds of conversion experiences throughout their lives. Conversions can occur through many experiences, it can be spiritual, mental, physical, material, etc. Whether it is something large or significant, or something so minor we might not realize it at first, everything we experience converts us in some way." He continued, "A family business such as yours has been a place where everyone that has had the opportunity to work there has not only had a conversion experience by deciding to work there, but also to remain there."

Dennis continued, "I believe every person that has ever come to your restaurant is converted in some way by what is so special about it, and everything the business and the people who embody it represent. The actions and the words of you and your staff represent what your values are, and those values subconsciously evangelize those you interact with." He concluded, "It's not a ministry where you stand at a pulpit and say things that drive people away; rather, what I call the 'Tate Ministry' is something deeply personal and conveyed in such a way that people are attracted to it. One example in particular is how the stories shared at the table with customers often include personal experiences that subtly showcase some form of conversion within the story while conveying an underlying teaching or life lesson that often results in the customer experiencing some sort of personal conversion."

As a leader, the act of self-conversion is directly correlated to self-transformation. "Transformation is the act of transforming or the state of being transformed while conversion is the act of converting something or someone" (Wikidiff. 2021). A leader willing to be transformed takes time to reflect on their words and actions through mindful meditation, analysis of who they are, who they want to be, what they're doing right, and what they could do better.

Every leader should envision themselves as the type of leader they would want to serve if they were in the position of those they lead. "Self-improvement is important for a leader so they can evolve in their leadership development and continue to develop skills across a range of areas that help build a stronger culture. When leaders begin to focus on self-improvement, this also helps with contributing a clear vision for the team" (Anne Tracy, 2021). Taking time for self-reflection and improvement develops three key leadership benefits that result in more effective leadership. According to leadership development advisor Beth Armknecht Miller, those benefits are:

- **Self-Awareness and Self-Regulation:** "Self-awareness gives you the ability to understand your emotions, strengths, weaknesses, drives, values, and goals, and recognize their impact on others you are leading. Self-regulation involves the ability to control or redirect your disruptive emotions and impulses and adapt to changing circumstances. Building these emotional intelligence components will improve your leadership" (Beth Armknecht Miller. 2021).
- **Integrity:** "Becoming clear on your core values will help to strengthen your leadership integrity and lead you to better decisions. Our integrity is often put to the test during stressful and difficult times. Taking time to review your key decisions and actions in the recent past and grading them against your core values is a good discipline for leaders. Doing this consistently can solidify your values and make the decision-making process easier in the future. Integrity will not only produce better quality from you, but at the same time it will increase your expectations of your team and encourage them to perform at the best of their ability" (Beth Armknecht Miller. 2021).
- **Confidence:** "Confidence is crucial for leaders. It helps in effective communications, decision making, and influence building. The more you reflect on your strengths and how you can build upon them, the more confident you will be as an individual and a leader. If you start to

doubt yourself, your team will start to doubt you as well, negatively affecting productivity and effectiveness of your team" (Beth Armknecht Miller. 2021).

One of our head servers, Shelby Henry, shared what daily conversion means to her and how she exercises it. She said, "No matter what may be going on in my personal life, I know when I come to work, it is all about work. When I am at work, my focus is on being the best teammate to my co-workers and the best server I can be." She continued, "If I'm training a new server, I have a responsibility to make sure she is converted into the server the restaurant needs and the server the customer expects. If I am waiting on a customer, I aim to give them the best dining experience they've ever had. If I convert someone from having a bad day into a good day simply because of my interactions with them, I know I have done my job, and I take pride in that." She concluded, "These actions would not be possible if I did not take time for self-reflection. It is important to me to take time to reflect on the good and bad of each day and allow those experiences to convert me into the person I desire to be. Allowing myself to reflect on my weaknesses gives me an opportunity to grow, and through that growth I am better equipped to serve the community and my loved ones, even through the most difficult of times."

Leaders are in a position of leadership to lead by example, making them responsible for the actions of their team, both good and bad. Effective leaders take time daily to evaluate their team's production with the purpose of enhancing their performance and job satisfaction. Equally important, the leader also must take time to evaluate their own production with intentions of enhancing their performance and leader-ship skills. Like St. Benedict said, this transformation takes time. It doesn't happen overnight. It takes commitment and dedication to continually take small, incremental steps daily, allowing you to transform and convert into the leader you aspire to be. This process is never-ending.

We should always aspire to become the best leader we can be. We cannot become content. We must always be open and willing to learn from others and our experiences, so we are not average leaders that do the bare minimum. We want to become a great leader that people find attractive to work with and for. This is all achieved through daily conversion of self. The ability to do so results in the strength to uphold the values embedded into the culture of that business or orga-nization. Again, those values serve as the "why" you're in business or in leadership. If your actions don't reflect those values, you are failing your team, company, and community.

In our business, my father and I take time daily to find a place where we can be alone and free of distraction to reflect on what we did well, what we didn't do so well, what we can do better, and what we need to do to be better. This is first and foremost the most important step in becoming better leaders. If we do not take time to reflect and focus on converting ourselves into the leaders we and our staff need, we are not leading effectively. From there, we evaluate the performance of our staff: who is excelling, who is having trouble, what actions do we need to take to get our staff to where they need to be, etc. If someone is having trouble learning a particular process on how to perform their job, we find new ways of training that best fits their learning style.

If someone is having a bad day, we find ways to inspire, motivate, and guide rather than belittle them and place even more pressure on them to perform without guidance, direction, or positive constructive criticism. We also encourage them to take some time to be alone, where they can clear their minds of any lingering thoughts or stresses and re-focus. We give them examples of how this benefits us and how it can benefit them as well. We continue to judge ourselves on our performance and turn that judgment into motivation to learn how we can become better leaders. This simple daily action of becoming aware of and reflecting on our actions and situations, learning from them, and using them as benchmarks for improvement results in long-term satisfaction and stability within the workplace.

A leader in any business or organization can easily implement this value into their culture simply by taking time daily to reflect on the strong points and weak points of their performance as a leader. A leader needs humility to accept the weak points of their leadership style and to use their judgment in a positive manner to learn and become a better leader rather than dwelling on weak points, holding them back from reaching their highest potential. Leaders also must accept the fact that the people they lead are not perfect either. As a leader, accept the fact that everyone you lead has strong points and weak points like yourself.

When judging their actions, do so in a positive manner. If they are having a bad day, mentally put yourself in their situation and have compassion rather than aggression. If they are struggling, approach them with support rather than discipline. If they are upset with you or someone they work with, assure them they can feel comfortable voicing their concerns to you, rather than judging them for their feelings and showing resentment toward them. When a leader takes time and initiative to do this, it becomes easier to praise your people when they perform well and take initiative to strengthen your people's weak points through guidance, mentorship, and training to turn their weak points into strong points.

CHAPTER 7

Obedience

———

"The virtue of obedience makes the will supple. It inspires the courage with which to fulfill the most difficult tasks."

—JOHN VIANNEY

Obedience. A word not commonly used anymore. Many of us may have heard of this word, but what does it actually mean? Obedience is defined as "the act or practice of obeying; dutiful or submissive compliance" (Dictionary.com s.v. 2021). A perfect example of this is expectations your parents or parental figures had for you as a child. Most, if not all, parents have their own unique and particular set of rules or expectations for their children. Some are stricter than others. As children, we do not fully understand why our parents say the things they do, why it's not okay to do the things they tell us not to do, why we can't do something we want to do, or why they react the way they do when we do or say something they tell us not to. All we know is we better listen to them or there will be consequences.

This act of complying with their rules or demands is true obedience. As we age, we become more conscious of our words and actions, as well as how they can impact those affected by their outcome. We begin to understand that our words and our actions will always result in either a good or bad outcome or sometimes both. Most importantly, we understand whether it is natural law, our religious beliefs, the laws of any political institution, academia, or the workplace; everything in life has a set of rules we are expected to obey, even if we do not fully agree with them.

Rather than being born with a reactionary state of mind like all other animals on Earth, we as human beings are gifted with free will. We use our senses, experiences, and knowledge to make our own decisions. We discover different things throughout life that attract us and things that send us in a new direction. The more attracted we are to something, the more energy, thought, and time we give it. We accept its flaws and focus on the long-term benefit of whatever it is we chose to remain obedient to. We put ourselves in environments we benefit from, as well as the ability to remove ourselves from an environment in which we suffer. Accepting that everything in life has its pros and cons helps give you a clearer focus and understanding of the top things that truly matter to you and you cannot live without. When you find a job or hobby that fulfills those needs, you remain obedient to the needs of that job or hobby, despite the potential vices or challenges associated with it.

"It is often forgotten that the root of the word obedience is found in *audire*, 'to listen'" (San Beda University. 2022). St. Benedict defines obedience as "putting into practice what is learned by listening to the other with the ear of the heart" (San Beda University. 2022). Not only must we hear what is being said, but we must listen with an open heart and mind and set aside our personal biases or differences, making an effort to understand why. St. Benedict calls on leaders to listen to the needs and concerns of those whose lives they impact and make decisions that benefit all rather than solely self. This is what keeps a leader in the position of leadership. If the leader is driven solely by their own motives, they become less influential and less trusted over time. Every person has both personal and work-related needs requiring attention.

If a leader neglects the recognition or responsibility of attending to their people's needs and only takes care of their own, their people will find another person to follow. A person's obedience to their leader cannot be forced or automatically expected because they are serving under your leadership; rather, true obedience is based on trust. Building trust takes time and effort. In their published article, *Journal of Leadership and Management*, Dr. Michael Urick and Dr. William Hisker share that St. Benedict challenges leaders to "always view his or her call for obedience within the context of never doing harm to his or her followers and always within the context of service." As a leader, if we aim to serve the people we lead, they in turn will be obedient to serving the needs of the business or organization to which they belong. In short, "Benedictine leadership and the right to call for obedience is evidenced by a leader's ability to listen, the knowledge of his or her obligation to service and a willingness to follow through on his or her obligations" (Hisker, W. J. & Urick. M. J., 2019).

How does obedience translate into the business world? It's important for leaders to consistently be obedient to the needs of their organization. More specifically, it's the leader's ability to effectively influence their team, dictating the results of their team's ability to complete their tasks or assignments. For example, when you adopt a puppy, you teach it simple commands such as sit, lay down, shake, etc. Teaching the dog commands is important to ensuring the dog remains obedient to your commands throughout its life. Humans are a little bit more complicated.

For a leader to achieve obedience from their followers, they can't just give orders they themselves wouldn't do. They must give the orders in a manner that influences their team to make the necessary decisions while executing their job responsibilities in a manner that brings out the best in them. An effective leader takes the initiative to be conscious of how they can influence their followers to not only obey instruction but present it in a manner that exhibits how that instruction will benefit the follower and the business. Even in high stress or pressure situations, humans can still think before they speak and make decisions they don't anticipate regretting. This action results in your followers being better prepared to make decisions that best align with yours—resulting in less micro-management.

"The term 'micro-managing' specifically refers to a leader who doesn't trust those around him or her, and thus, has to be involved in even the most minute decisions. Unfortunately, not only does this breed resentment in those being micromanaged, it results in exhaustion for the leader, and keeps them from looking at the big picture" (Bill Crawford.

2021). If a leader does not trust their followers to make decisions on their own, how can the business or organization continue to be successful in the long-term? It cannot. Dr. Bill Crawford provides us with two key principles that can help a leader engage their followers in a way that results in unleashing their followers' best potential while influencing them to be obedient to your leadership.

- First, ensure what you want them to do is good for them as well as good for you. Often, we are so focused on what we want to achieve that we don't stop to consider how this is going to be beneficial to those in our organization (or family). Knowing what is important to those we lead and how that aligns with what is important to us is crucial to effective leadership.
- Second, those who look to us for leadership must believe we both understand and care about them. You have heard the phrase, "People don't care how much you know until they know how much you care." Letting people know you understand their perspective (even, or especially, if they are concerned about something) allows them to drop the need to defend that perspective.
  - Bottom line, you don't want them to be in the "defensive brain" or the "resistant brain," and listening to learn what is important to them and letting them know you get it results in their willingness to hear what you say next.

Coming from a generational line of entrepreneurs, my father and uncle were fortunate to have learned from their father, grandfather, and uncles while working for their family's business. Throughout their lives, they witnessed and learned from successful leadership strategies and somewhat unsuccessful strategies, ultimately preparing them for the leadership positions to which they were destined. Even at an early stage in their lives, they anticipated to go above and beyond what needed to be done. Living with the expectations that their father would not only hold them accountable but teach them leadership at a young age. They may not have always wanted to do what they were asked, but they eventually understood there is nothing more powerful than the boss and their children playing their part in the operations of the business.

I, like my father, sometimes struggle with trying not to micromanage. It's not because we don't trust our team; it's because we are just extremely passionate about what we do—a passion so strong we feel we have an inherent responsibility to oversee every aspect of the business and its operations daily. We devote our entire souls and beings to our business and want to make certain every operation, interaction, and process is being followed the way we designed it and the way we need it to be. Sometimes that passion consumes us, driving us to the point of exhaustion caused from trying to handle too much on our own due to not effectively delegating tasks. As I mentioned in my introduction, some of the biggest reasons restaurants fail are due to absentee ownership, poor communication, and training.

It is important for a leader to be present in their business or organization and willing to help out where needed while delegating. Having a daily presence in your business better allows you to be obedient to the needs of the staff and the business. We have learned through trial and error that when we allow ourselves to delegate certain jobs or decision making to others, it results in either a positive or negative outcome. When they're positive, we thank the person responsible for the decision or action; thus leading to us to delegating more frequently. When they're negative, we use it as an opportunity to reflect on the decision or action made, its outcome, and what we can do to improve moving forward.

In short, micromanaging can be a natural tendency for people in a leadership or ownership position. The key to controlling the extent to which you micromanage is based on being present in your business or organization and making sure the people you hire and employ are aware of the company's values and share in those values. Once you've built a team with shared values and goals, creating and sustaining the opportunity for proper and continuous training of your staff allows you to effectively delegate. If your team is given the proper training and knowledge to perform job tasks, they will have the confidence and trust in themselves to complete their work the way you need them to. Once they do, you as the leader develop a deeper level of trust with that individual, providing you with a higher comfort and trust level knowing they'll execute their job responsibilities the way you need them to without you being directly involved.

In our business, we onboard staff that best align with the values of us and our business. Hiring staff with shared values is critical to the upholding of them. Hiring individuals that do not share in these values can potentially lead to future issues. We continue to build a team centered on mutual values and goals, and in turn, those values are present and attractive to the customer, leading them to not only return, but share the experience with others. Robert Barto, one of the loyal patrons for twenty-plus years, shared, "In the two plus decades I have dined at your restaurant, I have seen many new faces and several changes both internally and externally. One thing that has never changed has been my interactions with the staff. It is apparent that you and your father, as the leaders of your businesses, have remained obedient to upholding the values you live by, and the values you want your business to represent."

Robert added, "No matter what challenge you faced, you ensured you and your staff remained obedient to the values of the business. During the COVID-19 pandemic, you were obedient to following the health and safety measures put out by the CDC, allowing your staff to feel comfortable working and your staff to feel safe. I can agree that each of the values you mention in this book, you and your staff live by. The interactions I have with your staff members is a reflection of the leadership there." He concluded, "Sure, there may have been times where you and your staff had disagreements, but you guys never lose sight of being obedient to the needs of your staff, which in turn results in them not losing their obedience to their job duties and the needs of your customers."

Before, during, and after dealing with the challenges of COVID-19, we involved staff members in critical decision making, challenge them to think outside of the box, and break away from their daily job tasks that may at times feel like automation. As previously mentioned, involving your team in decision making makes them feel important and valued.

It gives them assurance that their leader trusts them and their ability to make decisions on their own without constantly having to get approval. Again, one of many key roles of leadership is to oversee the operations of those they lead. It is easier for my staff to identify more in-depth, micro-level problems within their job responsibilities which can sometimes be overlooked by my father and I. Allowing them the opportunity to be involved affects the way they perform their job and has been a critical part to our success.

We make a conscious effort to frequently ask them, what's your opinion on this? How can we make your job more efficient? Where are areas of waste in the way you do your job? What changes can we make to make our business's operations to be more efficient? What actions will best prepare us to deal with the future and overcome any challenge at hand? What can we do as leaders to best serve your needs? What needs have the customers voiced to you that we need to address? I know we have a problem but instead of dealing with it, how do you suggest we solve it?

Having to work both day and night shifts, our "hybrid" chef, Shawn Arford, is entrusted to making decisions daily. When interviewing Shawn on what obedience means to him in the workplace, he shared, "I have always been a believer of giving 100 percent effort in what I am tasked to do. It makes it easier when it is something you enjoy doing. I am trusted enough to make many decisions that affect how I perform my job. Anything from deciding what cooks to place in what position on the line, deciding on a weekend special, deciding how much food to prepare, suggesting a change, etc. I focus daily on being obedient to listening to others and making thoughtful decisions that best benefit the customer, the team, and the business."

Shawn continued, "Your grandpa taught Vickie and Patty how to prepare his recipes while working by their side. Their progression along with their commitment to their job and the business led to your dad and grandpa having them make many different decisions on their own. That level of trust was built through the understanding of each other's vision and goals for the business." He ended, "I now learn from Vickie and Patty. It has helped me know what kind of decisions to make and now I make decisions on my own. If there's a time when you guys make a decision I don't completely agree with, I'll still make an effort to understand it and continue to be obedient to my job duties. When you or your dad and I have a conversation about something in the kitchen, I am encouraged to make the decision I feel best. We both understand when I make decisions, I make them based on what's best for everybody."

Of course, there are times that test our patience or challenge our thoughts on what we should do or what we could have done, but ultimately letting them know we care about their opinions and concerns gives them reassurance that even though there may be times of difficulties and failures, we are all focused on the success and well-being of each other as individuals and for the business. Being open to their opinions and concerns, whether it is work-related or not, and making decisions as a team, reassures us all.

In times where we may not agree, we assure them we understand their perspective on the topic and thank them for making us aware of their thoughts, thus allowing them to let down their guard and feel more comfortable voicing their opinions. These actions have resulted in our staff having a greater sense of obedience to us, the business, and the people we serve. Equally important, it has given us a better sense of obedience to our staff. Having a vision is easy; having the obedience to follow through with what you believe in despite any challenge is when long-term stability and success become attainable.

Obedience is dependent on both parties involved hearing the needs of one another and fulfilling them. A leader can implement and achieve obedience in their business or organization's culture by consciously recognizing the difference between being a boss who gives orders or a boss who leads by example. I like to say a position will give you power and authority, but leadership will give others inspiration and passion, keeping you in that position.

I have realized if I am to earn the trust of my staff, I have to be on the ground working by their side, encouraging them when they're distressed, working together to solve issues, and shouldering responsibility for what happens in the workplace. If I am to simply give orders, stand back, observe, or not even be present, I not only lose their trust, but I will never receive their trust, especially when making decisions that affect them or their job.

I have listed below several keys to obedience we focus on in our businesses. I believe these small yet effective practices of obedience benefit anyone in a leadership position seeking to build a team mutually obedient to one another and the needs of their business or organization. Our obedience to these thoughts and actions has resulted in a more obedient staff, a decrease in employee turnover, increase in job satisfaction, and the ability to inspire our staff to become the best version of themselves.

- Attracting, retaining, and maintaining a team that collectively shares the same values as you and the values on which you built your business or organization.
- Allowing them the opportunity to voice their opinions and listen to their concerns. Both work related and non-work related.
- Reassuring them daily you appreciate the job they do, how much you value them, and how grateful you are to have them a part of your team.
- Allowing them the opportunity to use their discretion to make decisions that affect the way they perform their job.
- If they make a decision you don't agree with, let them know you understand why they made that decision and work with them to come up with a way to determine what would have been a better solution.
- Allowing them to be a part of operational changes made to the way they perform their job.
- Inspire them to think long-term success rather than short-term gain.
- Create an environment within your business or organization that gives them the freedom to be creative, give their input and feedback, and grow.

Applying these concepts was critical to the success of our business over the last thirty-eight years and counting, giving me the assurance that if you as the leader serve others before yourself, you will achieve a following obedient to you, the business or organization you all belong to, and the people you aim to serve.

CHAPTER 8

Discipline

———

"All success begins with self-discipline. It starts with you."

—DWAYNE JOHNSON

I'm sure we've all heard the word "discipline" throughout our lives, as well as applied it. Your parents may have said to you as a child, "You need to be disciplined to get good grades," or your coach may have mentioned, "If you want to get better, you have to be disciplined to your training regimen." Whether getting good grades in school, being competitive in sports, or earning a promotion at work, everything we set out to achieve has required some level of discipline.

Many successful well-known leaders, such as George Washington, Theodore Roosevelt, and Lou Holtz, have been quoted referring to discipline as being an important part of their success. We have heard this word, but what does it mean? Dictionary.com defines discipline as "an activity, exercise, or regimen that develops or improves a skill; training." When we discover something we thoroughly enjoy doing, we naturally form a discipline to make time for it, regardless of what is going on in our personal lives. When we realize we have a skill that needs improvement in a sport or in the classroom, we use self-discipline as the driving force for making time and effort to strengthen that skill.

Dwayne "The Rock" Johnson's quote fits the narrative of this chapter perfectly. True success begins with your ability to be self-disciplined to accomplish your goals. Though these successful people credit self-discipline as the driving force to their accomplishments, at some point they have had other people along the way who believed in their visions, goals, and aspirations, assisting them at some point in the journey to success. That is why true long-term success is dependent on your ability as the leader to not just influence others to believe in your causes, but to inspire them through your actions, mentorship, failures, and small achievements, showcasing your self-discipline to achieving the end goal while influencing them to not quit when things get hard and becoming self-disciplined themselves. That is when true long-term success prevails.

St. Benedict's perspective of discipline emphasizes the importance of having self-discipline. "The goal is to move from a discipline imposed from the outside to a mature self-discipline in which a person possesses a robust love of learning and, in setting his or her own goals, is able to imagine and pursue the steps necessary to achieve those goals" (San Beda University. 2022). Essentially, when we have self-discipline, we break away from outside distractions and redirect our energy and focus toward a goal we plan to achieve. The act of self-discipline and long-term vision for success gives a leader the commitment to persevere through any challenge life throws at them.

Self-discipline is a work in progress. It is a skill developed and strengthened throughout your life if you continue to practice it. Practicing self-discipline is similar to exercising; if you train a muscle consistently over a period of time, it becomes stronger, and the exercises used begin to feel more natural. You develop a routine so strong you can't find an excuse to break away from it. "A leader without discipline can make no true progress without an internalized willingness to commit oneself for the long-haul, a willingness to do the hard work of stretching beyond one's comfort zone mastering the complex skills necessary to move people and organizations to a more effective and efficient way of operating" (Hisker, W. J. & Urick, M. J. 2019).

The sayings "nothing good comes easy in life" or "to achieve great things, you must take great risks" convey the under-lying principle and value of discipline. When we develop a discipline for something we want to achieve, we take into consideration much more than just the raw definition of the word. Discipline requires having a long-term goal in mind and accepting there may be challenges to deal with along the way. On that disciplined path to success, we must allow our-selves to get out of our comfort zone and try something new or engage in something we have no experience in. Discipline requires we do not let failure deter us; rather, we embrace it as an opportunity to grow.

Life is like a roller coaster—full of ups and downs. The low points in the journey are meant to teach us a lesson, making the high points more meaningful. The high points give us a sense of gratification and motivation to keep working toward our goal. It is through the act of discipline that gives a leader the mental strength and stamina to get through the hard times, leading to the achievement of their long-term goal. "The self-discipline of a Benedictine leader becomes a model for others to emulate. The discipline of Benedictine leadership demands a long-term commitment to continual reflection and growth. That is why discipline will be evidenced through sustained hard work" (Hisker, W. J. & Urick, M. J. 2019).

The message St. Benedict emphasizes is an understanding that leadership requires releasing oneself from a discipline driven solely by motives to achieve personal gain and redirecting discipline to a focus of inspiring others to believe in their goals while working together. Rome wasn't built in a day, and I'm sure the empire would've never been built if it wasn't the shared vision of many. Though it only took one person to initially envision building the empire, it required that person to inspire a community of others to believe in their vision, to act on it, and to remain disciplined to follow that leader through the ups and downs.

If a leader exhibits their commitment to be self-disciplined to work hard toward a shared goal, it sets the tone for what the leader expects of their followers and gives them a standard of what is expected behavior to achieve their shared goal. It takes a dedicated and disciplined leader to build a vision and how to achieve it, but it takes a team to accomplish it.

In the article *Journal of Leadership and Management*, Dr. Urick and Dr. Hisker emphasize, "Self-discipline develops in you a set way for your thoughts, actions, and habits. Self-discipline means doing what needs to be done when you don't feel like doing it. It means that you accept the responsibilities and accomplish your goals...self-discipline implies self-management or self-control, self-motivation, self-reliance, self-confidence, and self-awareness and eventually, remains the basis for trust." A leader who accepts and applies these attributes becomes better at what they do because they hold themselves accountable to the success of their business or organization and the success of their team. A disciplined leader takes control of their emotions both good and bad, which will result in peace of mind and thought, no matter what happens. Whether it be in business, sports, school, medicine, etc., there is countless evidence proving effective leadership requires self-discipline.

A perfect example of this is a sports team. The head coach inspires and leads their players to work as a team and to perform to the best of their ability so they can achieve their shared goal of winning a championship. If the head coach is demanding and unmotivating, they will have a difficult time leading their team to a victory. The team can be disciplined to review film, study the strengths and weaknesses of their team and their opponent's team, and have every offensive and defensive play mapped out and instruct their team on what to do in each situation, but if the players aren't disciplined correctly, they will not win the game.

It is when the coach is disciplined and shows his commitment through hard work and training their players based upon their individual needs and providing them the tools and guidelines they need to help them succeed that they will begin to become self-disciplined to work toward the same goals as their coach. When they all are disciplined to work together through adversity, keeping on mind the end goal, they have the motivation to achieve it.

In our business, having self-discipline is one of the biggest reasons we have been successful for so long in the restaurant industry and a town with one red light. Self-discipline has gotten us through all of life's toughest challenges thus far. From the beginning stages of our business, when my father and my uncle first opened, having zero experience in the restaurant industry, it was self-discipline that continued to motivate them to be a success. It was self-discipline that kept them committed to the long-term success of their business, giving them the endurance to work fourteen- to sixteen-hour days, seven days a week until the mortgage was paid off; accepting the fact that if they were to be successful, they needed to be hands-on owners.

It was self-discipline fueling their fire to be community leaders and give back to society however they could. It was self-discipline that gave them the energy to continually go over to each table at which customers sat, taking a moment to introduce themselves and letting their patrons know they appreciated them and valued their patronage.

It is self-discipline allowing us the humility to take responsibility for any mistakes or failures we, our staff, or the business has made, using that moment of failure as a learning lesson to become better and working as a team to make our weak points, strong points. It was self-discipline that prevented them from squandering their money on any unnecessary items or goods, making sure what was made was reinvested into the business, and into the people that worked for them. It was self-discipline that gave us the confidence to reopen and build onto the restaurant after the fire in 1996 that left us closed for business for six months. It was self-discipline to remain open during the financial crisis of 2008 and the COVID-19 lockdowns in 2020, tenaciously persevering through the hardships of those times so we could continue to provide a stable work environment and source of income for our staff and ourselves.

It is our self-disciplined mindset that inspired those we employed to also become self-disciplined in committing themselves to us and our business, helping the business survive however they could. It was a self-disciplined belief in God that he was going to get us through any challenge we faced, taking time to pray for his guidance, strength, and peace in the good times and the bad, discipling ourselves to the service of his will and the service of his people. Living with self-discipline has gotten my family's business through a lot of tough times, leading to many joyful times. I am not here to talk about the successes of our business, but rather use them as a golden example of how leaders with no prior experience in their industry conquered challenge after challenge and remained prosperous through the daily practice of self-discipline.

Today, there are so many little details to remain conscious of. A few examples are the way the tablecloth and wrapped silverware are placed on the table, to inventory control of even the smallest items like coffee creamers, and ensuring our staff is performing the way we need them to. In moments of fatigue or stress, you cannot abandon it, leave it up to someone else, or give up on it. We need to be involved with the operations of every department of the business and have a daily awareness of what's working and what's not. We must stay disciplined to get up in the morning and put in back-to-back long days of work if need be.

We are disciplined to engage with our staff and customers even in times where we may not want to be bothered—disciplined to make sure our staff is trained properly and continue to progress disciplined to make time for prayer and meditation. No matter how busy we get, we make a small amount of time for reflection daily, even if it's only five minutes. When we break away from being pulled in many directions, it allows our subconscious to process anything we may have trouble with and gives us a more rational solution to the issue at hand.

Having a business is like having a baby—it won't survive unless it is taken care of by people who care. It requires your full attention 24/7, 356 days a year. From its inception, you must take care of every little aspect of the business; as it grows and matures, it becomes more autonomous and self-sufficient, but to ensure its longevity, you are still always there for it, regardless of what may come up in life. To that point, parents, like leaders, need to make time to be alone and reflect. If you don't make time for yourself and neglect your needs, you won't be able to perform the way you're needed to. Like a child, growing and developing a business takes time and effort, but what dictates its success is it's leadership.

We acknowledge that we cannot allow our personal life to negatively affect our leadership. We remain self-disciplined to cancel out distractions or deterrents and remain focused on the health and well-being of our business. Self-discipline motivates us to get up in the morning, knowing that many people's livelihoods depend on us. It continues to provide a quality product at an affordable price. It helps us work hard and be attentive to the needs of others while building, developing, and motivating our team.

The self-disciplined leader must have a constant optimistic outlook on the future with no fears of the "when ifs" and the "what ifs." It gives them motivation to pursue their goal when times get tough. Their resilience builds confidence in themselves and from their followers in their leader's ability. Trust is the foundational principle that a leader-follower relationship is built upon. If the leader cannot earn the trust of their followers, their followers will leave them for another leader who can.

One of our head servers, Shelby Henry, shared, "When I come to work, I remain disciplined to make sure that while I'm here, 100 percent of my attention is on work no matter what's going on in my personal life. I remain disciplined to provide the customer with the best customer service experience they have ever had, especially if there is a time where I am waiting on someone who's being difficult. To that point, I remained disciplined to learn the needs and wants of my customers and went above and beyond to make sure their dining experience is one to remember." She said, "I stay disciplined to keep an open mind to new ideas or processes. Even if I don't fully agree with it or understand it, I know it will affect my job, so staying open-minded has always helped me grow. When we had our first point-of-sale system installed, it was the first time I had ever used one. I didn't know anything about it but was determined to learn how to use the hand-held device to take orders and was optimistic about how it will make my job easier. It was definitely a learning curve, but remaining disciplined to the long-term benefits of it made it easier to embrace."

Shelby concluded, "It is clear you and your dad are disciplined to make sure every customer and employee leave this restaurant happy. You guys have been great with leading by example and giving us pep talks that remind us to be disciplined to certain things that can leave a positive or negative affect on the business. You guys don't just speak about staying disciplined to our assignments and how to engage with the customers, you put your words into action and set a great example for all of us. That also helps us understand the way you and our customers expect us to perform our job, and I appreciate that."

We know the importance for a leader to be self-disciplined, but what actions can you take to acquire and strengthen these skills? An article titled "The Importance of Becoming a Self-Disciplined Leader" (Journey to Leadership, 2019) provides leaders with seven habits and mental practices proven effective in transforming a leader into a self-disciplined leader.

1. **Mind Management:** Mind management is centered on the ability to understand your emotions at all times. Once you understand your emotions and what causes you to

feel or react the way you do to different situations or conversations, you can control them. You naturally begin to think before you speak or act, breaking the instinct to instantly react. With this ability, you become more conscious of how your response will affect you and others while giving you greater control.

The following mental practices are designed to help us develop stronger mind management:

- Nurture your mind with empowering thoughts. While working, remove distractions from and block social media sites.
- Train your brain to handle both positive and negative outcomes.
- Meditate or turn to religion. Meditation brings a sense of contentment, and religion helps us relinquish our problems and emotions to God.
- Forgive yourself for past mistakes and let go of grudges and regrets.

2. **Emotional Intelligence:** Emotional intelligence is fostered when you learn from your mistakes and those of others so you may be better prepared to handle whatever situation you are presented with. Emotional intelligence is the result of being conscious of your emotions and their potential outcomes, not letting them dictate your decisions, rather, being conscious of the outcomes of those emotions if acted upon. Emotional intelligence emphasizes blocking our negative emotions and embracing a positive mindset when handling stressful or difficult

situations or people. The following mental practices are commonly used to discipline your emotions:

- Identify habits you consider undisciplined and those that reflect your values and goals.
- Change your self-dialogue.
- Cultivate gratitude to transform negative circumstances into positive ones.
- Abstain from vain entertainment.
- Limit your social circle to individuals who possess the qualities and skills you desire.
- Sleep a healthy number of hours and don't hit the snooze button.

Maintain a healthy diet and exercise regularly.

3. **Self-Awareness:** Self-awareness is centered upon being aware of your strengths and weaknesses. An effective leader must take time for self-evaluation, allowing them to recollect on their weaknesses and have a willingness to strengthen them, rather than letting their weaknesses deter them. At the same time, it is important for a leader to not let their strengths get to their head and go, rather share your strengths with others and allow them the opportunity to learn from you with intentions of strengthening their weaknesses. It is beneficial to find people that inspire us, but we must remember everyone is created different in their own way. Not one person is identically the same. We must be conscious of accepting the guidance we seek while not disbanding what makes us who we are trying to become.

The following commonly used mental practices help you become more naturally self-aware of your actions as well as your strengths and weaknesses:

- Invest in your personal growth and don't allow obstacles to mentally set you back.
- Recall what you did well and with pleasure in your childhood.
- Determine what immediately and sustainably attracts your attention.
- Read books to gain and expand your knowledge.
- Hire a professional to help identify and employ your strengths.
- Seek the truth about yourself and don't be afraid of failure.

4. **Time Management:** Throughout our lives, there has probably been at least one instance where either your parents, teacher, or coach has mentioned you need to be better at managing your time. Time management is becoming aware of your daily, weekly, monthly, and yearly tasks and organizing/preparing your schedule to make the most of every moment of every day. Your time on Earth is limited; having a plan and making the most of every day provide a solid path to accomplishing whatever it is you are set out to achieve.

The following commonly used practices help you become better with time management:

- Define achievable, specific goals with timelines and deadlines.

- Do not procrastinate, find excuses to postpone your work, or allow anyone to distract you and waste your time.
- As you increase in leadership responsibilities, carve out some time to execute tasks that matter and recharge your batteries.
- Have consideration for other people's time.

5. **Character Building:** Throughout our life, we face many ups and downs. The one thing we have in common is an opportunity to learn. An effective leader views the results of both good and bad experiences as an opportunity to grow, giving them the life lessons needed to transform them into the leader they aspire to be. Each of these experiences builds character. Rather than letting the low points in our life dictate our outlook for the future, let them serve as a source of resilience. In moments of success, do not boast. Allow that experience to serve as a source of reassurance in moments of difficulty. Hold yourself and others to a higher standard.

These disciplines will allow you to make decisions with confidence while allowing you to hold yourself accountable for your actions. Be thankful for the experience. Be willing to learn from trial and error, other people, books, and any other sources of information you feel are compelling and beneficial. Building character is a life-long process that originates with the intention of becoming the best we can be and the best leader our followers need us to be paired with the acceptance to learn from our mistakes, which is then built upon our life experiences and how we cope with them.

The following commonly used practices help you build better character:

- Stay true to your values.
- Don't be discouraged by our failures. Resist the urge to give up.
- Read, listen, and watch things that motivate you. People of faith can turn to their belief systems to stay on track.
- Draw learning lessons from your mistakes rather than regret.
- If you don't have anything good to say, don't say it.

6. **Relationship and Team Building:** Building strong relationships with dedicated team members and those you provide a service to is one of the most critical factors to maintain long-term success as a leader and as an organization. The stronger relationships with your team members result in greater trust between leader and follower, as well as the ability for the leader to entrust more micro-level decision making to their followers without constant oversight or intervention. Strong relationships with the people you serve result in repeat business, referrals, loyalty, networking opportunities, etc. Making time to know your team and patrons on a personal level will pay priceless dividends.

The following key practices have proven effective in relationship and team building:

- Define your responsibilities, avoid stepping on anybody's toes, and delegate tasks as needed.

- Treat your team members as adults and show them respect.
- Place equal importance on the best interests of the company and your team members.
- Promote self-discipline among your team and encourage innovative ideas even if they fail.
- Share your performance expectations with your team and help them achieve their goals.
- Address unacceptable behaviors immediately without immediately punishing or humiliating the perpetrator(s).
- Avoid taking your job for granted or taking credit for the team's success. Stay humble.

7. **Execution, Motivation, and Structure:** At this point, you have dedicated time and exerted energy into becoming self-disciplined. You have a vision, you have a plan, AND now you're ready to put it into action. Through these experiences, you're able to offer predictability to the outcome of your plan, consistently motivate yourself and others while developing the structure of your vision and bring it to life.

The following key principles further ensure your action plan has structure, accountability, consistency, and the opportunity for improvement and growth:

- Share your discipline and attention to detail with others and help them pick up the slack without micromanaging.
- Don't impose your discipline on anyone else.
- Follow through with your ideas and finish what you've started while tracking your progress.

- Execute your plan in silence, and respect yourself enough to come through on your promises.

CHAPTER 9

Humility

"Humility is not thinking less of yourself; it's thinking of your-self less."

—C.S. LEWIS

Take a moment to reflect. Can you think of a time when you were so determined to be right in a situation even if you knew you were wrong? Can you think of a time when you were so adamant about doing something your way, that you wouldn't even consider welcoming the opinions of others on how the task should be handled? I can say I have, and I'm sure you have too at some point in your life. Thinking back on those moments, what was the outcome? Did you prove to yourself and others that you were right? Or in the effort of trying to prove you were right, were you proven wrong? Did you succeed doing things the way you wanted or did it result in failure?

Whether proven to be right or wrong, how did you react at the outcome? Were you boastful or arrogant when proving to yourself and others you were right? Did you causing others to feel resentment or favorability toward you? Were you spiteful and envious of the person who was right when you were wrong? Regardless, most instances such as these usually result in the experience of humility. What is humility? Merriam-Webster defines humility as "freedom from pride or arrogance: the quality or state of being humble." Interpreting the word based on its definition alone can sound like a negative quality until it is applied to something—especially leadership. When we act with humility, we earn the respect of others. You may wonder, how is thinking of myself as less important and beneficial to leadership? Let me explain.

Humility is essentially the most important value any person should have, especially leaders in the eyes of St. Benedict. In his book of rules for his Benedictine Monastery, he dedicates an entire chapter to explaining what humility is, its importance to our overall well-being, and twelve steps to help the reader live with humility, then tying the teaching of humility into many of his short stories throughout his book of rules. St. Benedict's definition reflects words from scripture: "For all those who exalt themselves will be humbled, and those who humble themselves will be exalted" (BibleGateway. 2021).

We know what humility means, but it is important to know what "exalted" means to understand this phrase. According to Merriam-Webster, exalted means "held in high estimation: glorified or praised." This powerful quote wants us to understand that those who consider themselves powerful or held in high regard to others without the testament and support of their peers shall learn humility the hard way, through failures and misfortunes.

Contrary to this, if we are to be exalted by our peers, we must humble ourselves to think less of ourselves and more of others. We must have an understanding that we are not better than anyone else and believe all humans are created with equal dignity. We must have a willingness to admit mistakes and ask others for help when we don't know the right answer. In our successes, we must not be boastful or greedy. Give credit where credit is due and let your actions be your voice. These kinds of actions incentivize others to hold you in high regard.

"Benedictine leaders must be willing to understand that, although they are called to a leadership role, they are no better than those who follow" (Hisker, W. J. & Urick, M. J., 2019). To this point, we as leaders must set a high standard of acceptable and unacceptable actions and behaviors. Rules and regulations are created to preserve law and order. Without them, chaos and eventual demise of the organization you lead is inevitable. We lead by example. If we make special exceptions for ourselves or a select few, we lose our credibility and trust as a leader, resulting in others breaking the rules or removing themselves from your leadership. "Leaders without humility begin to think that they are special and the rules do not apply to them. Without a ground in humility, destructive forces of pride can corrode leadership skills. For leaders nothing is more dangerous. Pride of person, place or position has been the historical downfall of many" (Hisker, W. J. & Urick, M. J. 2019.).

A business or organization can have the best product or services in their industry and that success is usually credited to the leader. A leader without humility selfishly and graciously accepts the credit and recognition of their business's or organization's success while forgetting to share their fortunes with the people that helped their company or product generate the success it has. A leader with humility gives credit to the members of their business or organization when being recognized for their success, in addition to using whatever resources are available to incentivize and reward their team.

It is important for a leader to encourage working as a team to create solutions to problems rather than just giving commands. Don't give an order you wouldn't do yourself. At the same time, having the humility to accept that the actions of your followers are a reflection of your leadership. If we as leaders cannot accept our faults, make special exceptions for ourselves, or don't lead by example, how can we expect the people we lead to act any differently? We must not only take accountability for our actions, but the actions of others. In moments of failure, we must take credit, even if we aren't directly tied to that failure.

A humble leader makes the conscious effort to lift the spirits of their followers when they experience failure. To remind them, "Hey, a mistake was made that didn't give us the results we wanted. Rather than dwell on the past and what you should or shouldn't have done, let's focus on what we can do moving forward. Let's take this failure as a learning lesson and use it to create a basis for improvement. In moments of individual failure, humble leaders identify what their weaknesses are and place others in a position that best allows them to use their strengths to complement our weaknesses."

"Benedictine leaders who are disciplined by humility recognize their gifts matter only in relation to the gifts of others. There is a strong orientation of service—a willingness to recognize and develop the skills and talents of all who contribute to the common cause. Benedictine leaders measure their status in the flourishing of those who follow and the development of the leadership potential of those who will be called to leadership in the future" (Hisker, W. J. & Urick, M. J. 2019).

Knowing St. Benedict's definition of humility, how does it translate into the business world? An article from the *Harvard Business Review* written by John Baldoni provides us with a great correlation. "A sense of humility is essential to leadership because it authenticates a person's humanity. We humans are frail creatures; we have our faults. Recognizing what we do well, as well as what we do not do so well, is vital to self-awareness and paramount to humility." The lesson of humility we learned from St. Benedict translates perfectly into the meaning of humility for business leaders. We acknowledge that we are not perfect, and we have our own strengths and weaknesses. It takes the collective efforts of every individual in the workplace to combine their talents, complimenting each other's weak points with each other's strong points, to successfully accomplish their shared goal.

Humble leaders use their position as an opportunity to delegate in a manner benefiting all rather than self. They recognize their team's skillsets and create opportunities for them. When we openly admit what we don't do well and allow our team's skills to improve it, we truly showcase our humility. It is important for leaders to accept their weak points and inspire their followers to have a sense of freedom within the organization by encouraging them to voice their opinions.

This action shows your followers you are human and not above them just because of your status or title. Let them know you have flaws and strengths just like everyone else and that it takes the collective work of everyone within the organization to achieve the goal you share in the most efficient and effective way possible, encouraging top-down, bottom-up communication throughout the business or organization.

In my family, humility is a leadership trait taught and expected of us throughout several generations. Since my ancestors immigrated to the United States and began their entrepreneurial aspirations, up until this present day, humility was one character trait never lost and always highly prioritized. No matter our status within the community and within our businesses, we never exalted ourselves or considered ourselves to be more important than others. We believe that through our hard work and the many blessings we receive, we are to use the fruits of our labor to serve God's will.

Having our faith, we have been raised on the belief that all men and women are created in the image and likeness of God. We are brought into this world with equal human dignity, honor, and respect. The moral value of humanity and valuing others' existence made it easy for us to view, respect, and treat our employees the same, regardless of their title, socio-economic status, race, religion, or any other discriminatory characteristic. We understand great things can be achieved for many when we reinvest in our people rather than solely ourselves.

We welcome differences, knowing that even though we are created equal, we are also created with our own strengths and weaknesses, making us all unique in our own ways. This sense of inclusion made everyone we hire feel included and accepted in our business. We allow ourselves to become vulnerable with our staff in times of difficulties, sharing our concerns with them; asking for their opinion assures them we too are human and have our own struggles. It gives them a deeper sense of trust in us, and they feel appreciative that we are comfortable confiding in them—fostering a relationship deeper than just boss to employee.

Showing vulnerability has made it easier for our staff to become vulnerable when we need them to, giving them the opportunity to be open to whatever suggestions we have and finding ways to incentivize them to become better than who they are today. It reminds them that the only person they should be competing with is themselves; that is the only way to truly grow.

One thing my father said that really stuck with me is, "We have seventy employees with seventy different personalities." The underlying meaning to this is though we must treat them equally, we must realize their differences call for a difference in how we approach them. Everybody responds to things in their own unique way. Using the same approach for everyone may work for some but not for all. Some people you can speak bluntly to, and others may require a more delicate approach. To understand the most effective approach to take with those we lead requires time, patience, understanding, the ability to envision ourselves in their position, an open mind, and the ability to make ourselves vulnerable.

Whether it be group pep talks or one-on-one chats with our staff, we commonly allow ourselves to become vulnerable by sharing our own vices or struggles. Our vulnerability exhibits humility. When we as the business's leaders share our vulnerability with someone on our team, it gives ground to relatability and shows we too are human. When sharing these stories or examples, we express how we believe we are meant to use them as a learning lesson and remain focused on what we can do to improve upon them, allowing us to continue pushing toward our end goals.

When the COVID-19 restrictions abruptly hit with no warning, we were taken by surprise and unsure what changes we'd make to adjust to these new restrictions, having never faced a challenge like this before. We turned to the staff to ask their input and suggestions. We collaboratively gave our input to ensure success within every department and the overall business. We credit our staff for our success during the pandemic and make sure they and the customers are aware when they congratulate us or ask how we did it. Each one of us knew our role within the business, and we executed our job responsibilities as best as we could, leading to our success throughout the many challenges faced.

Clear communication of their roles and responsibilities made it easier for them to execute their job the way we needed them to, so the customers can continue to receive what they expect. Having never dealt with the kinds of challenges we faced during the pandemic, none of us, including my father and I, had the exact answers needed in order to sustain our business. Having understood this, it required the humility of ourselves and our staff to acknowledge that we may not know the solution now, but we would work together, communicate daily on what's working and what's not, and use our collective gifts to create solutions to these problems. We took time to promptly acknowledge and address problems to grow individually and as a whole. Every staff member understood if we didn't work together through this, we ran the risk of failing.

We were all committed to making it through the crippling restrictions and made whatever adjustments necessary in order provide a living for each other and quality, home-cooked food to our customers (our external family, as we like to call them). Most importantly, we constantly express how grateful we are to have them and for the great job they do. People like to be acknowledged for their work and contributions. Many organizations today lack this simple yet effective gesture. Genuinely thanking your staff for being a part of your team and giving credit where credit is due reassures them that their work is meaningful to us and our patrons.

Being in a position of leadership in our kitchen, our hybrid chef, Shawn Arford, has proven how having humility is critical to success in leadership. Shawn said, "Humility must be present in every part of your life in order to have it in leadership. Leadership isn't always easy, but it's necessary for someone to step up and lead by example. Having humility makes leadership easier...I know being in charge comes with more responsibilities. If someone doesn't know how to do something, I know it's better to take time to teach rather than criticize. If someone is struggling, I know it is better to help them than to let them continue to struggle. I acknowledge the strengths and weaknesses of my co-workers and adapt what I do to best help the team. I understand that if I can train the other guys on the line to do everything on the line, no matter who's in what position, we can get the job done."

Shawn continued, "Staying humble usually isn't the easiest thing to do, but I know it is always the best thing to do. If someone is acting in a manner that challenges my humility, I understand the best way to solve whatever issue may arise is to take into consideration all the variables and put myself in a position to solve it, rather than complain about it and do nothing." He added, "Having a boss that acts with humility sets a good example for the rest of us. If he is unsure of how to do something or what decision to make, he asks for the help of myself and others. If we are really busy and need help, either you or your dad are always the first ones to step in and help out wherever is needed rather than let us struggle, regardless of whatever else you may need to do. If there is a problem with a customer or staff member, you find a way to fix it so it doesn't happen again instead of pushing it under the carpet. I have experienced through many situations both good and bad that having humility will always give you better results."

We exhibit humility in our engagements with our customers as well. When we hear positive feedback, we thank them and don't allow it to get to our heads or make us too comfortable. If they compare us to another business and criticize the flaws of another business, rather than agree with them, we share that we're sorry to hear about their bad experience and thank them for making us aware because it gives us another thing to focus on maintaining so they don't have that same experience with us. When we hear negative feedback, we welcome it rather than resist it. Instead of ignoring or making excuses for why the customer had a negative experience, we thank them for making us aware of the problem and offer ways to make it up to them.

We take everything into consideration. Even if we think we're right, we still acknowledge that the customer is always right. Throughout our existence and especially during the pandemic, we encourage feedback from the community we serve. Rather than thinking we have all the answers to best serve their needs, we go directly to the customer and ask them for input on what we can do to best serve them. This allows us to better fulfill the needs of the customer while reassuring them they are valued and their voices are being heard, resulting in the continued loyalty and commitment to patronizing Luigi's.

I am not the only person who can attest to these actions. Kathleen and Bob Millward have been patrons of ours since our origins. When speaking with them, they shared, "What other business owners, specifically restaurant owners, take the time to go around and talk to every single customer and genuinely enjoy doing it? The only place we have experienced this has been Luigi's." They went on to say, "That gesture really goes a long way with people. I know it means a lot to us and other people we know that dine there. Regardless of your or his own self-interests or if you're not in the mood to go around and spend time talking to others, you guys have shown humility by going around and talking to everybody—even sharing personal stories that help you find common ground with the customers...We know if we have any suggestions or concerns, you guys are always open to hearing them and try to make decisions that place the interests of the customers first."

As Dr. Robert Hogan puts it, "Humility in leadership does not imply the absence of ego or ambition. Rather, humble leaders are better able to channel their ambition back into the organization, rather than use it for personal gain." A web article written by Sherrie Campbell on entrepreneur.com gives business leaders key personality traits that, if consciously put into action daily, will enhance an aspiring leader's ability to exercise humility in their words and actions:

Humanity: "We are all human, and therefore, all flawed and vulnerable in our own unique ways. Great leaders have a depth of understanding, garnered from their experience, as to where their inherent strengths and weaknesses lie" (Sherry Campbell. 2017).

- Having self-awareness of your strengths and weaknesses is vital to your success as a leader. You cannot always be right, and you cannot always have things only your way to remain successful as a leader. If you give off the perception you believe you're perfect and not flawed to your followers, they are bound to leave you for someone else. Effective leaders and followers alike respect when someone they work with allows them to become vulnerable, admits they have flaws and are not perfect, and seek the help of others they work with. Vulnerability creates authenticity and allows for stronger connections between leader to follower, and follower to follower within the organization. It results in a sense of acceptance of one another and our flaws as well as trust from one another to allow others to coach and mentor them to make their weak points strong, fostering the opportunity for self-growth and improvement.

Balanced authority: "When humility is present, leaders act more like a 'player's coach.' Their position of authority is used to establish order and discipline between team members. These leaders are on the front lines helping their team to know, understand, and pursue their individual and collective goals" (Sherry Campbell. 2017).

- As a leader, it is important to maintain law and order within your business or organization. A humble leader successful in the long-term does not use their authority in a manner resulting only in self-centered ambitions of success. They do not use fear, threat, or shame tactics to get what they want. Humble leaders accept themselves as equal human beings to their followers. They communicate their weaknesses.
- Leaders who allow themselves to become vulnerable often result in their followers becoming vulnerable, expressing to the leader what they need from an individual and organizational standpoint to become a better person and team member. They take responsibility for the performance of their followers and their growth within their business or organization and find ways to inspire their followers to be the best they can by giving them a voice, allowing them the opportunity to grow into the person they desire to be

and the person you need them to be in the organization. It is a win-win situation.

Promote others: "Promoting others is done to better the person, and to enhance the overall effectiveness of the collective organization. Because they lead from humility, they have a natural understanding of the bigger picture; the more successful the enterprise the greater its leadership" (Sherry Campbell. 2017).

- Promotion in praise, job title, or pay rate are all an expectation every follower has within a business or organization. A humble leader promotes and incentivizes their followers to work hard. Hard work is a demonstration of the follower's commitment to the success and well-being of the business or organization they serve in. A humble leader recognizes their followers' hard work and allows them the opportunity to be promoted to a higher position/positions where they may be in more of a leadership role within the business or organization.

Acknowledge others: "Humble leaders understand the importance of acknowledging when something didn't work. They coach their team members individually and collectively on what went wrong, they develop new strategies, and send their team back into the field to try again. If the team went wrong, humble leaders know they were a part of that equation. Humility breeds humility" (Sherry Campbell. 2017).

- In addition to this statement, it is for humble leaders to acknowledge the existence of the people they lead. To greet them by name and not wait to be greeted by them.

To ask them how their family is, if everything is okay in their personal life, and is there anything we can do to help them inside and outside of work.

Collaborative: "Success is better gained from a mindset of collaboration rather than competition. Collaborative leadership views team members from a place of equality, with each possessing their own set of skills. Each player is coached to best serve their specific purpose, role and assignment on the team" (Sherry Campbell. 2017).

- A humble leader is not competitive with their followers in deciding who is right and who is not and what is the right way to do something and what isn't. Instead of competing, a humble leader again accepts they are not perfect, nor do they have every single answer or solution. They welcome the input of their followers to collaboratively find a plausible solution to a problem, or a new innovative way of accomplishing tasks.

Good sport: "When being led from humility, team members know that losing one battle is not indicative of losing the war. It is through great loss and sometimes even great tragedy that teams and businesses have the greatest opportunities to improve, grow and thrive" (Sherry Campbell. 2017).

- It is important for leaders to understand that in business, sports, or life, there will always be moments of failure and success. It is important to graciously accept failures as reasons to be better and areas to improve upon, never giving up hope in themselves and their followers; rather, motivate their followers to think the same way. In times of success, it is important to share in that success with the team, rewarding them in whatever way is appropriate, and show gratitude toward themselves and their followers, encouraging them to do the same.

Integrity: "Leaders who operate from humility did not build their reputation on a set of false, loud, flashy pretenses. They do not seduce others with fancy words not backed by subsequent action. These leaders are people others can depend upon. They do what they say, and say what they do" (Sherry Campbell. 2017).

- Humble, successful leaders preserve the integrity of their values they build their business upon. They do not waver from those values in times of success and failure. They live those values by putting them into action on a daily basis. There is nothing that can shake a humble leader or make them waver from their motivation. They are honest in their actions and words and attract like-minded followers.
- The humble leaders ensure everyone is clear on their roles and responsibilities, including themselves, ensuring the team the leader has built achieves the desired success.

Grateful: "Those who lead with humility welcome differences. They value what each person brings to the table and are thankful for the diversity each person adds to the team…[w]hen it comes to accomplishments, humble leaders are always more grateful than prideful" (Sherry Campbell. 2017).

- It is important to explain the difference between prideful and grateful. A prideful leader boasts of their success, even if it wasn't solely their efforts that resulted in the success as a leader. A humble leader is grateful not only for their success as a leader, but to their followers for committing themselves to the business or organization.

From my experience and the research, I can attest that a leader of any business or organization can take these same key principles listed above and put them into practice daily to become a humble leader. Exercising humility in your leadership style is proven to result in:

- Experiencing and developing a more accurate and positive view of themselves and others.
- Acknowledgment of prioritizing the needs of others rather than solely your own will benefit all within the organization, helping you all succeed on a personal level and as a whole within the organization.
- More naturally appreciating others and their contributions.
- Giving credit where credit is due when you are successful and not boasting of your own success.
- Increasing self-confidence as a leader having earned a deeper sense of trust from your followers and the people you serve.
- A healthier, well-functioning, highly effective team that sticks together creating long-term success.

CHAPTER 10

Stewardship

———

"We make a living by what we get. We make a life by what we give."

—WINSTON CHURCHILL

When John F. Kennedy famously stated in his inaugural address, "Ask not what your country can do for you; ask what you can do for your country," it made a powerful impression on everyone who heard him speak that day, the people who read it in the newspaper, and those who read about it in history books today. He began his presidency by challenging every American citizen to find and act on ways to positively contribute to society. The challenge he tasked us with is more important today than ever. Today, it is common for people to experience instant gratification, entitlement, selfishness, and greed. Having the mentality that if it is good for me, I'm going to do it—giving little to no thought on what the outcome of that decision may be and how it could affect others.

This kind of mindset has only proven to eventually lead to long-term failure in life. Believe it or not, we are born with the instinct to serve others. "Our brains are wired to connect with others using mirror neurons. Through these specialized nerve cells, our empathy is activated, and we feel the emotions of others. This circuitry connects our brains with every personal encounter we have. So, our bodies are naturally compassionate" (Terri Kozlowski. 2020).

Throughout life, we all encounter traumatic situations that happen to either ourselves, someone we are close to, or even events we hear about—all of which bring out a feeling of compassion and a desire to help however we can. We experience this same feeling of compassion when either ourselves or someone we are close to has a reason to celebrate. We desire to share in that celebration with them. For example, when your favorite sports team wins the championship, you become filled with joy and want to celebrate that success.

Compassion goes hand in hand with stewardship. What is stewardship? It is "the responsible overseeing and protection of something considered worth caring for and preserving" (Dictionary.com. 2020). In other words, stewardship means to serve. A steward leader asks their staff and patrons what they can do for them and the company, especially in times of a major crisis like COVID-19. Being naturally born with compassion, we are also born to exhibit stewardship toward something we care about or value, serving the needs of those people, communities, or natural resources affected by our decisions.

Though compassion and caring comes naturally for things we like or enjoy, so does the instinct to prioritize the things that benefit you, even if it has a negative effect on someone or something else. In leadership, there is an inherent responsibility to place equal concern on what benefits you and the resources you impact in your life. There are extreme examples where you choose what's best for yourself. What's most important to leadership is your stewardship to every resource in your life. Stewardship in leadership has a calling even greater than this; to give back however you can, and impact as many lives as you can. Get involved in a local non-profit or your local borough or school board. We cannot allow the allure of wealth and status to lead to greed and sin; rather, use it as a tool to help the greater good of the organization, the community, and the world.

From a Benedictine leadership perspective, St. Benedict calls leaders of all backgrounds to make decisions based on how it will benefit the common good, rather than just benefiting ourselves. "The Benedictine worldview holds that all creation is a gift of a loving God and, as such, must be handled with the deepest of respect and care" (Hisker, W. J. & Urick, M. J. 2019). St. Benedict calls us to find value in everything in this world and to do what we can to sustain its purity, preserving it so it can last for generations—thus benefiting the common good of all humans and nature on this earth. I like to say, "Karma is a reflection of your actions." The older I get, the more truthful it is. If we make a conscious effort to make good decisions and a positive impact on someone's life, the more likely it is for good karma to come our way.

One small example I can share with you are times where we have a staff member who needs a ride to work. The easy thing to do would be to say, "Sorry, I can't help you. You're going to have to find a ride or miss work." Rather, my father and I are willing to give these individuals rides. It's a win-win situation. The employee gets to work and doesn't have to worry about losing hours. In return, we don't have to worry about being shorthanded and we help them in a time of need. In leadership, understand that every person, place, and thing you oversee requires your undivided attention, commitment, and most importantly, your love. Your level of commitment to your resources is a reflection of how much you truly care for them. Parallel to care is understanding their needs. If you understand what keeps your resources sustainable, you are better prepared to fulfill those needs.

Making decisions that benefit the common good have led to long-term sustainability in our business, giving me the reassurance that if you do the same, your job will become more fulfilling. "The Benedictine lattice of leadership requires a firm commitment, on the part of leaders, to the effective and efficient stewardship of the resources entrusted to their care. From this, there arises the duty on the part of leaders as good stewards not to let the human, fiscal, and physical resources under their care go idle" (Hisker, W. J. & Urick, M. J. 2019). These resources include more than just the business or organization you lead and the people that work for you. These resources include your family and friends, every person in the community you reside in, and every aspect of nature within your community.

There's an old saying along the lines of, "If you have two apples and someone needs one, give them an apple." The underlying message is to be willing to help others however you can. Do unto others as you wish to be done unto you. We have been born with a moral obligation to the preservation of everything created on this earth. It doesn't matter how much you give—what matters is that you gave something. St. Benedict calls leaders to use their God-given abilities to serve with compassion and mindful consideration for the long-term well-being of these resources so they may not succumb to waste or failure.

This trait is particularly important in business leadership. St. Benedict's definition is interrelated to the definition of steward leadership in business. Steward leadership is defined as "a form of leadership that focuses on others, the community and society at large rather than the self" (Full Sail Leadership Academy. 2020). To be an effective leader, make decisions and actions that reflect your compassion toward the well-being and success of your followers and the people you serve. This important attribute can make or break your business or organization. A leader lacking stewardship can still achieve success, but only in the short-term.

There are many examples of business leaders or members of a business or organization that have not practiced stewardship, followed their own greedy desires, and only amounted to short-term success and long-term failure. Some of the largest cases of corporate greed resulting in a massive amount of financial loss, business failure, or demise are cases like the billions of dollars in account fraud committed by the leadership at Enron. Investor Bernie Madoff who was convicted of the largest Ponzi scheme in history, and Washington Mutual's leaders convicted of billions of dollars in mortgage fraud. These cases are examples of how these businesses and their leaders gave into the greed stemming from their success and prioritized serving their own selfish ambitions over the needs of the common good in which they are in business to serve!

Some of the most successful companies both large and small prioritize the stewardship of their employees and the people and communities they serve. One example of a business who exercises stewardship well is Stanley Black & Decker. Their business strategy is built upon the stewardship of people, product, and planet. Their leaders implement programs to better the livelihoods of their staff through the opportunity to receive additional education to further enhance their skills, resulting in employee loyalty and empowerment. They focus on the stewardship of their community by developing products that aim toward becoming carbon positive, reducing landfill waste, and using sustainable and reusable resources. These acts of serving the common good are the root cause of their continual growth, sustainability, and long-term success.

"Community building, responsibility, and trust within an organization all hinge on these nine components" (Full Sail Leadership Academy. 2020). A steward leader's values direct their goals and visions, and they make the effort to criticize and master acting according to their values, while attracting and building a team with the same. From there, the steward leader takes the initiative to serve and hear the needs of those they lead, addressing them with genuine compassion and acceptance.

Making necessary changes as needed to preserve their team and their values, motivating them to continue to focus on their shared goal. They become vulnerable with their followers, seeking their advice and input on any decision making or actions they may not have the answer to. They take risks by welcoming new ideas on new ways or implementing applications to achieve their goals. Nothing great comes without risk. This risk taking always ends with results; if they're negative results, use them as a learning lesson and move on to the next idea. If they are positive, use them as a benchmark of actions taken in the right direction.

In our business, stewardship is one of the pillars of survival in the restaurant industry. Serving others is the top priority. Not just generic service, get in, get out, on to the next one, but personal, intimate, compassion service that exhibits you truly care about the needs and wants of those you serve. More importantly, if we want the results we expect from our staff, we must treat them the same way. We have built a team that shares our values of going above and beyond the call of duty to take care of our customers. When my father and I take the initiative of getting to know our staff on a personal level, they feel more comfortable and accepted at their workplace.

When we focus on their strengths, we encourage and motivate them to keep doing the great job they're doing, as well as allow them to use their discretion in decision making that affects their performance. When we focus on their weaknesses, we do it in a manner that opens the window of opportunity for personal growth and development, so they are better equipped to serve.

We at Luigi's place a major emphasis on hospitable and accommodative service for every customer that dines at our restaurant. From the moment they walk through the door, they are greeted with a smile and asked how we may serve them. Once attending to their needs, we make them feel comfortable by making conversation with them, getting to know their name, what they like to drink or eat, and remembering that whenever they come back. Unlike most other restaurants, if the customer asks us to make something special that we don't have on our everyday menu, we are happy to accommodate if possible.

One of our managers, Daniel Patton, has been a great example of a steward leader. When discussing what steward leadership meant to him, he shared, "It is equally important to me as it is to your family that every guest and employee that comes through our doors is treated like family. If an employee needs a ride, I am happy to give them one. If a customer requests something we have as a special but don't have on the menu, or makes any other special request, I do my best to accommodate it." He continued, "If a customer or employee is feeling down or something is bothering them, I listen to them with a compassionate ear, and offer to help them however I can."

One of our other managers, my aunt Mary, is known for her generous and hospitable stewardship. "The simple things like honesty, hard work, kindness, compassion, fairness, and hospitality go a long way in life and in business. I view my coworkers as family and would do anything for them. Same thing for our customers! I am so proud of both what our staff and customers bring to Luigi's, making it what it is today." She continued, "We strive to be a place where people come to be treated like family. I never hesitate to do whatever I can to help someone. Whether that be a family member, coworker, customer, or someone in the community. At

Luigi's, if someone needs something, there is always someone here willing to help or give back. The values instilled in my siblings and I from our parents live on in this restaurant and everyone who works here."

David Osikowicz, a patron of ours since our origins, has continued to return to Luigi's with new customers for decades because of the Luigi's stewardship. I asked David if he could provide a few testaments of how we live up to the meaning of stewardship. This is what he had to say: "I knew Luigi's was going to be a success after my first time there shortly after you guys opened. At the end of our dinner, my friend had asked the server if you guys have any ice cream. It was her first day, so she wasn't sure and had to double check. She came back to the table and said, 'We have chocolate, vanilla, and strawberry, but if you'd like a different flavor, we'll go down to the grocery store and buy the flavor you'd like.' Needless to say, we were impressed by the level of stewardship we were given and from that day, Luigi's became one of our all-time favorites."

He continued, "From my experience in business, when someone is willing to offer that level of stewardship, doing whatever they can to accommodate the customer's needs, there is no reason they shouldn't be successful. Luigi's is one of the very few businesses who go above and beyond to accommodate the customers' needs, resulting in people driving from all over the place to experience that, since it is so hard to find anymore."

Another example David shared was during the time we were temporarily closed due to the fire. David said, "My wife, Debbie, and I's twenty-fifth wedding anniversary was approaching. The restaurant was still closed at the time, so I called your dad and asked him when he planned on reopening. He said in a few weeks or so, so I asked, 'Well, how would you like to do a trial run? Would you consider doing dinner at my house to celebrate our wedding anniversary?' Your dad said, 'Of course, I'll bring a couple chefs and servers over.' Patricia, Paulette, and Kim Bobak were all there." Knowing the workaholics my father and uncle are, David agreed to this under one condition: that my father, uncle, and their wives join them as guests. My father and uncle agreed and had an amazing time with the Osikowiczs and their guests.

David concluded, "With only a couple weeks left until your reopening, your dad could've easily said they couldn't do the job and you had too much preparation to do. Instead, he and your staff were willing, excited, and grateful for the opportunity to come to our house, prepare the food there, and serve us all, knowing how much we love Luigi's and wanted to celebrate our anniversary with your food."

Patricia has a fond memory of this as well. She shared, "When I got the call to do this job, I was so excited. I got to finally get back to what I love doing: cooking for people. I made everything that day, from stuffed hot peppers, Chicken Maria, Eggplant Parmigiana, even made the sauce right there in their kitchen!" She continued, "After making the dinner and serving them, we were invited to stick around for dessert and coffee. What we did for Dave and Deb that day meant the world to them and to me. I have always been a believer in doing whatever I can to accommodate the customer's needs. If I can do it, even if it's something off the menu or if it's busy,

I am willing to do it. This industry is based on the value of service and hospitality, and we all try to give the best that we can."

It's easy for us to be attentive stewards to the people, places, or things we care about, but it can be challenging to be a faithful steward to everything your business or leadership impacts both directly and indirectly. The Full Sail Leadership Academy provides leaders with a list of components that build and develop a steward leader. If we act on these values, we can develop into the best version of leadership possible. This list is called *Nine Essential Components of Stewardship in Business*, which include:

- **Personal vision**: An acknowledgment of your values, morals, purpose, and goals. What motivates or incentivizes you to do what you do in your life.
- **Personal mastery**: Growing in the values, visions, and ambitions you personally hold through commitment, perseverance, and knowing yourself.
- **Shared vision**: Building a team or community based on shared values and goals.
- **Mentoring**: Training, guidance, and support from leader to follower, allowing for self-growth and empowerment.
- **Vulnerability and maturity**: Allowing yourself to become vulnerable with your staff, showing compassion, and finding ways to relate to them. Accepting things you don't have an answer to and humility to seek the help of others when needed.
- **Valuing diversity**: Accepting and welcoming diversity of ideas, experience, race, and ethnicity.

- **Experimentation and risk-taking**: Openness to the idea that there is a better way to do things. Accepting your failures and allowing your team members to be included in decision making.
- **Raising awareness**: Making others aware of concerns, difficulties, or failures within the workplace, as well as acknowledging others when they achieve success and celebrating with them.
- **Delivering results**: Everyone within the organization collectively putting their minds and efforts toward achieving a common goal, delivering the results you and your customers want.

CHAPTER 11

Hospitality

———

"Motivate them, train them, care about them, and make winners out of them...they'll treat the customers right. And if customers are treated right, they'll come back."

—J. WILLARD MARRIOTT

When you experience new places or people, how do you want or expect to be treated? Most of us would probably agree we want to be welcomed with open arms, greeted in a way that makes us feel comfortable, and assisted or helped when needed. When others take actions to make us feel or experience these things, they show hospitality. So, what is hospitality? Hospitality is defined as "the quality or disposition of receiving and treating guests and strangers in a warm, friendly, generous way" (Dictionary.com s.v. 2020). Acts as simple as greeting a stranger or someone you know with a smile and a hello are a small act of hospitality which typically goes a long way to most people. This gesture tends to transition into greater acts of hospitality, such as inviting them to events or gatherings, introducing them to friends and family, helping with something they're in need of, and the list goes on. The act of hospitality is contagious, driven from person to person.

When you are treated with hospitality, it makes you feel happy, welcomed, and appreciative. In turn, you subconsciously base your actions on hospitality because of how it makes you feel when someone is hospitable toward you. Whether we are the ones being treated with hospitality or the ones treating others with hospitality, it gives us a sense of fulfillment and a sense of satisfaction and pleasure, knowing we had made a positive impact on someone's day, or that someone else made the initiative to make a positive impact on our day. We show hospitality in our homes, our workplace, or other public places. How is it an important skill for business leadership? Let's start with St. Benedict's take.

"Any guest who happens to arrive at the monastery should be received just as we would receive Christ himself" (Hisker, W. J. & Urick, M. J. 2019). For Christians, we are raised to believe we are all born in the image and likeness of God, as well as to treat others how we want to be treated. With that being said, Christians should have the belief that we welcome everyone we encounter as Christ himself. From a non-religious standpoint, this quote can be interpreted as the act of showing an ample amount of acceptance and stewardship to everyone we encounter, just as we show anyone else we hold in extremely high regards, including how we expect to be received by others.

St. Benedict calls on us to "put aside individual plans and pre-occupations in order to let the unexpected person in, to help them get established, to respond to their most pressing needs" (San Beda University. 2022). St. Benedict reminds us of the importance of letting go of our humanistic desires and temptations blinding us to the needs of others while pursuing our own plans or goals. Yes, there are more extreme examples where you prioritize your own plans or pre-occupations over anything else—weddings, funerals, graduations, etc. The true meaning behind the quote is that we welcome others the way we want to be welcomed.

A personal example I can share is if I have a new employee on their first day of work. Rather than sending them to their new position and letting someone else make the first impression, I put my plans aside to make sure I introduce them to their co-workers, review their job responsibilities and requirements, show them around, as well as address any concerns or questions they may have or need for work, and most importantly, let them know if they ever need anything, work-related or not, I am there for them. For anyone, specifically leaders, treating others with hospitality always results in a greater bond of loyalty, commitment, and solidarity from those you impact. "For those leading in a Benedictine tradition, hospitality demands that they have a clear understanding of the core value of the dignity of every person as created in the image of God" (Hisker, W. J. & Urick, M. J. 2019).

To be effective, a leader must first and foremost have a clear understanding of what their core values are. A hospitable leader puts those values into action by acknowledging all human beings are created equal, regardless of our differences, and treating others as equals. Once you have an understanding and acceptance of this, it becomes more natural to treat others with openness, acceptance, and stewardship, not just for the betterment of them and how it makes us feel, but because it is the right thing to do.

So how does hospitality, particularly from St. Benedict's standpoint, intersect with its importance to leadership? Jan De Jong wrote in an article on November 21, 2018, that individuals in a position of leadership need to reflect on the meaning and purpose of what's called hospitable leadership. Jan wrote, "Successful leaders in hospitality demonstrate a leadership style that not only enables and inspires and sets strategic direction, truly welcoming input and viewpoints from operational staff and leadership levels that report to them, but also empowers those echelons and gives them due care and compassion, combined with a level of increasing self-direction and autonomy. This requires not only able leadership, but also calls for a suitable set of values and characteristics to be possessed and upheld by leaders."

The message Jan wants us to understand is that individuals in any position of leadership need to recognize that the people they lead reflect their values and every detail of how the organization is operated. Staying true to your values will dictate your feelings, thoughts, and actions and help build a team on a foundation of shared values, with knowing what's acceptable behavior. Effective hospitable leaders need to place a special focus on their hiring process. Having systems in place to properly vet and interview applicants to ensure that their values align with yours is critical. Values are a representation of personality traits. A hospitable leader needs to attract and retain others who share similar interpersonal skills, including resilience to stress, maintaining composure and confidence under pressure, critical thinking, patience, and of course, empathy.

For example, let's say it's a busy day of work at the restaurant and you're in a situation where you multitask. You have customers waiting to pay, waiting to be seated, tables needing to be cleared, and people on hold on the phone. In this situation, a hospitable leader understands how to prioritize what situation needs the most attention first, while delegating actions to other team members. While making these decisions, control your emotions and make rational decisions. You cannot allow the stress to get to you and cloud your thought process and decisions. Your team will feed off your words and your actions, so maintaining a positive and composed personality helps others behave in the same manner.

After addressing the pressing issues, you become aware of a customer complaint. Instead of ignoring the complaint or relaying a message to the customer from the server, a hospitable leader goes over to the customer themselves. Even if you believe the customer's complaint isn't legitimate, you still must thank them for making you aware of the complaint, don't make excuses for their bad experience, and present an opportunity to make it up to them. Your team needs to be trained to react the same way you do, in both good and bad situations. This action of hospitality is the difference between someone returning to you again for your services or never coming back and sharing with others their poor experience.

In business, hospitality is a critical skill successful leaders must acquire for success. "The overarching goal for everyone in hospitality leadership is meeting and exceeding the needs of guests. Business leaders emphasize the value of exceptional customer service in achieving guest satisfaction, repeat business, and excellent word-of-mouth advertising through social media and review sites like TripAdvisor" (Courtney Capellan. 2015). A hospitable leader places the needs of the customer first and foremost. Their whole team needs to make sure every person patronizing their business is treated like family and is greeted with warmth, friendliness, and generosity—no matter their appearance, background, or social status.

The hospitable leader takes time to understand the needs of their team and their customers while continually exceeding those expectations. "The example of shaping an inclusive work environment and showing respect for a wide variety and types of guests who the hotel establishments are welcoming, where diversity is embraced—but, importantly, all this not only applies to its guests, but also its workforce" (Jan De Jonge. 2015). These actions develop an understanding that for long-term success to be achievable, you must employ people that share in your values and personality traits. Once attaining your team members, continually act with hospitality toward them and their needs. Your team reflects how they're treated and in turn, will also show hospitality toward the people your organization serves. A team aligned in values and focused on the same end goal leads to the long-term success of the organization.

My aunt Mary, who's assisted us as a manager for close to twenty years, described Luigi's work environment as "[a] place where everyone who enters its doors is welcomed as family. A sense of kindness and warmth is radiated throughout the restaurant. We make sure everyone who leaves this restaurant leaves with a happy heart and a full stomach, with the thought in their mind, 'I can't wait to come back.'" She said, "We pride ourselves on fairness, honesty, and transparency. We do more than just acknowledge the presence of our staff and customers. We let them know we appreciate them and their contributions. We enjoy the opportunities to form friendships with our co-workers and our customers. Getting to know a little bit about their life and having an opportunity to give back brings us all joy. Whether it be our staff or our customers, they know that when they come to Luigi's, they will be treated with humbleness, thankfulness, kindness, fairness, appreciation, and most importantly, like family. That is what keeps our staff here for as long as they are and what turns first-time customers into regulars."

From a customer perspective, Jeff and Linda Zinkham shared the hospitality at Luigi's for the twenty-plus years they've dined with us. They highlighted, "When we walk in, we're acknowledged right away. We are even given hugs by you and some of your staff. We're taken care of right when we walk in. Your staff knows where we like to sit and try to accommodate it. Several different servers will come up to us and say hello, see if we need anything, and even engage in meaningful conversation. Everybody's so friendly and we're treated like family."

Jeff and Linda concluded, "You and your staff know our names and the names of many other customers. Every staff member we have engaged with has always been very hospitable and has gone above and beyond what we expect them to do because they want to make sure we have the best experience possible. I know this treatment isn't exclusive to us because we see you and your staff give the same kind of treatment to everybody else in the restaurant. You don't receive that kind of treatment from most places you patronize, and receiving it here means the world to us."

Joe and Marybeth Marcoline have been patrons of ours since our origins. When I asked their opinion on how hospitality is present in our business, they replied, "The Tate family possesses strong core values embodied in the entire staff. Every staff member models the behavior of their boss, and there is no job the owner wouldn't do himself! Even clean the bathrooms!" They continued, "Hospitality is expressed in the care and kindness the welcoming the family and staff give to every single one of their patrons. Hundreds of staff have come and gone since you first opened, but one thing has never changed—the family feeling every single person is treated with goes to your restaurant."

Joe and Marybeth concluded, "The staff make a conscious effort to make sure every person is taken care of, even if they are not our server. You welcome parties of families and friends and share in their celebrations. If there is a birthday, several staff members come out and sing and give a free piece of dessert. If there is a group in for a funeral lunch, you share in their sorrow and find a way to give back to the family. If a customer requests a dish you don't have on the menu, you're happy to make it if you can. These actions have built you a loyal and growing customer base since you guys opened."

One of our head servers, Shelby Henry, shared how being hospitable is one of the core focuses of how she performs her job and how it benefits not just her, but the business and the community. She said, "Hospitality is the essence of the restaurant. When people decide on where to go to eat, they want to go to a place that not just has good food, but good service as well. They want to go somewhere they feel welcomed and taken care of. I know that's what I want, so that's what I provide. I take pride in getting to know my customers and their preferences. I like having their drink and appetizers at the table when they arrive or going over to other tables and talking to the customers, even if I'm not their server. They come in as customers and leave here as friends."

Shelby went on, "My goal is to make sure if anyone is having a bad day, I will do whatever I can to turn it into a good day. I know hospitality is the key to that. Hospitality is something the Tate family values a lot, and it shows in the way they treat me, my co-workers, and the customers. They are always there to lend a helping hand if we need something and consciously reward us for our hard work or reward customers for their continued support. If one of my coworkers is ever in need of something, I appreciate the opportunity to try and help however I can."

It is evident through the claims of both our patrons and staff that the value of hospitality is a continually sought-after personality trait. Whether we personally desire to be more hospitable or receive hospitality from others, hospitable people deliver results that make people feel welcomed, appreciated, and return to you for your services. This value is proven to be a fundamental part of our long-term success. Valuing people more than profit continues to result in more than just a financial gain, allowing our propelled success as a business and as a community.

If you are new to leadership and aspire to become a better hospitable leader, Boston University provides some key actions:

Establishing shared beliefs, values, and goals: Like St. Benedict mentioned, the key to hospitality requires cultivating an openness to being transformed by an idea, a person, or an experience, as well as having a clear understanding of what their values are and how they put those values into action. A hospitable leader builds an organization of individuals who share their values. Those values shape the vision of the organization and its culture, achieving their mutually shared goal by putting them into action. The values of the leader and their employees build their vision for their business purpose and their goals.

- This is priority number one. As a leader, you must serve the needs of your staff first and make sure their values are aligned with yours. Once achieving that, you and your whole organization are prepared to accomplish the goals and visions you have for the organization and the people you serve. You cannot achieve your goals or efficiently serve without having your whole team centered on the same values.
- Having hospitality promotes followers to feel welcome within the organization with their strengths and weaknesses, differences, and allows them the opportunity to give input on how they can achieve their shared goals. Equally important, hospitable leaders welcome it, acting upon the feedback and using it to enhance their services.

Modeling by example: Effective managers provide instructions, guidelines, and templates for their staff. Effective leaders go beyond that and lead by example. They put themselves in the same position of those they lead and show through action how they are expected to behave and how to perform their job duties or responsibilities. "An important part of being an effective leader is educating others on what the organization stands for and why it matters" (School of Hospitality Administration Boston Hospitality Review. 2018).

- They ensure these values are upheld by keeping others accountable by truly living and acting in accordance to those values. "Great leaders effectively translate intention into reality by acting on the values they teach and the things they say to those around them" (School of Hospitality Administration Boston Hospitality Review. 2018). Acting on the value of hospitality encourages those they lead to also act with hospitality and builds trust in your company.
- When everyone in the organization acts with humility, it positively affects the customers and makes them feel welcomed, appreciated, and wanting to return for your services, generating a long-term commitment between leader and staff, and organization to the community they serve. It results in long-term commitment from staff to the organization, and long-term patronage from the community.

In addition to this, Larry Stuart, the author of *Hospitality: How to Add the Missing Ingredients Your Business Needs*, shares four traits that companies with the highest level of hospitality share. Those include:

- The highest hiring standards are adhered to.

- The training budgets and quality standards are mandatory and respected as part of the company's core values.
- Monthly, quarterly, and yearly evaluation practices are followed and appreciated by all staff members because they feel valued and important as the brand representatives that uphold the company.
- A feeling of empowerment, initiative, and purpose helped drive the guest experience to the highest level because of their entrepreneurial efforts.

CHAPTER 12:

Community

"Some people think they are in a community, but they are only in proximity. True community requires commitment and openness. It is a willingness to extend yourself to encounter and know the other."

—DAVID SPANGLER

What does community mean to you? At some point in our lives, we have all been a part of some type of community, whether it be our workplace, volunteer group, religious organization, sports team, your neighborhood, support system, etc. What does the word truly mean? Why do we find ourselves within certain communities and not others? Dictionary.com defines community as "a social, religious, occupational, or other group sharing common characteristics or interests and perceived or perceiving itself as distinct in some respect from the larger society within which it exists." A community is formed when we interact with others with shared attitudes, interests, goals, personalities, cultures, and hobbies. The community can be based out of one geographical location or in many parts of the nation or world. It can be in a brick-and-mortar building or online.

All communities are built to attract those sharing something in common, giving us a feeling of inclusion among that group. Within this community, friendships and other relationships form. We bring our individual skills and talents together and use our strengths to achieve a common objective. We find jobs that interest us and stick with organizations aligning with our values. We seek out others in times of difficulties or sorrow. We pray with others when searching for peace. We choose to live in a community with others we share commonalities with or things such as a safer neighborhood, better schools, less taxes, closer to work, etc. We naturally draw like magnets to communities providing the necessary resources to fulfill our needs and wants.

On the contrary, if something occurs within the community we do not agree with, we end up leaving to find another one built on the same interests as ours. It is in our human nature to build relationships and dwell with like-minded people. We are not meant to be isolated or to do things on our own. All great things or events in life have been accomplished by the collective work, efforts, desires, and ambitions of a community of people, even if the leader of that community takes or is given most (if not all) of the credit.

There have been many successful people in the short term, but they fail in the long term because they lose their sense of community within the organization. They prioritize their own success and status over the well-being of the organization and the people who embody it. This community's health is maintained by the leader properly attracting others with the same attributes and weeding out the ones who do not. They aspire to help others within their community reach their highest potential rather than using them as pawns to help them get to where they want to be. "Social life is not exterior to the human being but part of the human's essential character—an individual can only grow and realize his fullest potential in a healthy community" (Libertatis Conscientia: AAS 79, 1987, p. 567).

St. Benedict reinforces these claims by stating that leaders are meant to build communities serving the common good of those within it and outside of it through their actions and initiatives. "Individuals must be given respect and dignity and can never be harmed or treated as objects to advance the interests of a particular community. Yet at the same time, an individual's self-interest cannot be pursued to the detriment of the common good" (Hisker, W. J. & Urick, M. J. 2019). Who wants to belong to somewhere that doesn't give you the basic respect and human dignity you deserve? No one.

We are attracted to particular places for many reasons. The deeper-rooted cause is because the leaders give the people within it respect and human dignity.

"A Benedictine leader understands that the social nature of human beings is not uniform and calls for fostering an organizational climate that respects diversity of ideas, healthy social pluralism, and a commitment to renewal and change, while preserving a deep respect for historical traditions and a sensitivity to particular customs and locals" (Hisker, W. J.

& Urick, M. J. 2019.). While a community is formed by individuals who come together with shared values, interests, and goals, the long-term sustainability is dependent on the leader accepting different ideas and opinions on what the community should do, and how they should do it when making decisions that dictate how and when they all accomplish their common goal(s). All members of a community, particularly the person(s) in charge, must acquire the ability to accept the fact that as life progresses, places, people, politics, social norms, technology, etc. changes.

Recognizing these changes and adapting to them by embracing change is an opportunity to be better at what we do and how we serve each other within the community and outside of it. At the same time, respect the values and customs that built that organization and never drift away from them. Even with changes in leadership, leaders and followers within the community must maintain its values, for this is the root cause of stability and long-term success for your organization's community—reinforcing the point of "Benedictine leader's commitment to community will be evidenced through teamwork, reverence to tradition, and a commitment to positive organizational change" (Hisker, W. J. & Urick, M. J. 2019).

So how does St. Benedict's view of community and its importance translate into the business world and business leadership? To start, simply put, a business is a type of community. "It has a social identity, a set of values, a shared mission to solve a problem and often also a sense of place" (David Spinks. 2016). When an entrepreneur starts their own business, it is built upon a set of values that structures the norms and purpose for its existence. It has a mission, goal, or objective meant to solve a problem or serve a public need or want. From there, they build their business's internal community by employing other individuals with the same values and interests or goals. They then continually focus on the health, well-being, and personal development of the individuals within their business's community.

This action is required. If you cannot fulfill the needs of your team, they will inadequately fulfill yours. Attending to your internal community's needs will only strengthen your business, allowing it to grow and harvest a stable opportunity to continually benefit others both within your internal and external communities. You may be wondering, what is an internal and external community? How are they important to each other and how do they differ? Let's start with the internal community.

Thanks to her web article, Veronika Mazour provided five key reasons why having a healthy internal community within your organization is important:

It serves as a natural support system: "A strong internal community is your support system. It's a group of people who believe in your brand and will defend you" (Veronika Mazour. 2018).

- It serves as a place your employees feel comfortable seeking help when experiencing difficulties either at work or at home.

Information sharing: "Your community members can drive their own networks to your community, resulting in more customers or users" (Veronika Mazour. 2018).

- Your employees or current customers may share your business or services with other people they know, allowing your customer base to expand.

Talent development: "You can call on your internal community members for feedback on your product, testimonials, and ideas" (Veronika Mazour. 2018).

- You create and implement systems for collecting feedback from employees and customers. This allows them a secure and private opportunity to voice their opinion on what you're doing well and what you're not doing well.

Innovation: "Most companies rely on org charts and hierarchies. As a consequence, employees are placed in boxes where they interact with a limited number of people, mostly related to their own field of expertise. Internal communities allow to escape this structure and form cross-department groups where employees from different backgrounds can come together and interact. Great ideas are often born in just such a type of interaction and mingling" (Veronika Mazour. 2018).

- Putting in operational systems allow you to collect the voice, opinion, and ideas of your staff, allowing them to become a bigger part of the organization and make an impact on the operations of the business as a whole, rather than their specific department, resulting in innovation and advancement.

Employee Satisfaction: "Social Interaction and recognition score highly on the Maslow pyramid of human needs and its employee needs equivalent" (Veronika Mazour. 2018).

- There are four common ways for leaders to foster employee satisfaction within their workplace. Those being flexibility, giving generously, investing in technology, and providing on-going training and mentorship.

Our internal community is built upon ideals our team shares in and lives by. A community that's purpose is to serve others better than our competitors. A community where our people enjoy coming to work, feel appreciated, given the opportunity to voice their opinions and ideas and have them accounted for in decision making, and the opportunity for self-development and growth through charismatic, compassionate, and servant leadership. If your values and goals don't align with the internal community in which you serve, how can you adequately serve others? You can't.

My family's restaurant business has built an internal community of people who first and foremost share in our standards and our vision. Our values serve as the root cause to our actions, and our actions reflect our values. Having those shared values results in similar interactions or performances in pursuit of our shared goal—welcoming all guests with quality homemade meals with prompt service where customers are treated like family.

Building upon that, our staff typically either enjoy working for a family-owned business where they are treated like family, work for someone who notices their contributions, work with other people and a boss who cares about their personal life and needs, work in a fast-paced environment, enjoy and appreciate the opportunity of networking with first-time and repeat customers, or enjoy the opportunity to make and prepare food dishes from recipes handed-down through generations of my family (some of which they had when they immigrated here from Italy).

We understand a work-life balance is not just for us but for each one of our staff members. We emphasize flexibility in scheduling and requests off. We try our best to accommodate each of our staff's needs and requests. We encourage them to take time to do things for themselves, whether that be a hobby, vacation, or just a day for relaxation or prayer.

It can be easy to get burnt out putting in too many hours at work, especially one fast-paced with high intensity. Providing our staff with the ability to work around their schedule allows them the opportunity to refresh, recharge, and refocus and results in their efficiency at work and, most importantly, high employee satisfaction.

Life is constantly changing, so we must be open to change and opportunity for growth from an individual and organizational level. We find more efficient ways to operate and more beneficial ways of addressing and solving employee needs and concerns. The one thing that never changes is the values, ideas, and cultural norms embedded into the business, serving as our "why" on a daily basis.

The internal community my family has formed at Luigi's has attracted all walks of life for thirty-eight years and counting. The one thing knitting us all together is each person has a sense of belonging fueled by our shared values, interests, and goals. Building and sustaining a community such as this has been the key to low turnover rates and high employee satisfaction.

From an employee perspective, Paulette Geisel provided examples of her experiences within our internal community and how it's attracted, benefitted, and retained her for decades. She shared, "Everybody has a story, an issue that they're either currently dealing with or have had to deal with. We all have issues no matter who you are. I believe everybody needs to be heard and being heard can provide the strength and support they need. Your father has been and continues to be there for his people. He doesn't look at his staff and laborers or work horses, he views them as himself, as a person with a soul. No place or job is perfect, but the environment of empathy and human dignity created in your restaurant made it a desirable place to be."

She continued, "There have been times where someone is struggling with something, and your father has always been there to listen to their concerns. He could've brushed them off, not cared about the personal lives of those he employed and told them not to bring their personal life into work, but he didn't. He was concerned about the personal well-being of everyone he employed, and it showed by the way he treated people when they needed someone."

Paulette added, "If someone needed a ride to work, he'd give them a ride. If someone was short of money, he'd lend them money without keeping tabs, if an employee wanted to be trained to perform a different kind of job in the restaurant, he'd honor their request and allow them to be trained. If an employee had an emergency at work, he'd let them leave. I don't know if I know any other business leaders who'd act in the same way. The community within Luigi's is built upon caring for one another as self, and that's what kept me at Luigi's for as long as I was. I had someone from another restaurant offer me a management position and I denied the request with no regrets, knowing I don't want to leave a job where my boss and my co-workers care about my well-being as much as they do at Luigi's."

She highlighted the inclusiveness of our community by mentioning, "I remember your father hiring someone who had a mental and physical disability—someone most people probably wouldn't hire due to their limitations. That wasn't true with your father. He found a job for that man and never gave him more work than he could handle. He treated him with the same respect as he would with the wealthiest customer to come in, or anyone for that matter. I can remember a time when a girl was a dishwasher and wanted to become a server. She was dealing with oral health complications that affected her appearance and her personality. Louis said to me, 'Paulette, you have a more delicate way of handling this kind of situation, would you mind relaying a message to her for me?' 'Sure,' I said, and I proceeded to talk to her privately. We discussed her current health complications and I told her we wanted to promote her to a waitress, but we had to address her oral health first and your father was willing to help her pay for the work she needed done."

While Paulette shared this, I realized the positives that came out of this situation. For the staff member, she had a boss who understood her needs, wants, and concerns and was willing to help fulfill them. For my father, not only did he retain an experienced employee by offering a promotion and financial assistance to correct her health issue, but he upheld the standard of appearance and personality he had for his staff. To many other business leaders, this action may have not been taken, or if it was, be viewed as a burden. To my father, he understood the importance of maintaining a community of compassion and human dignity and found ways to embolden and inspire his employees.

Paulette concluded, "Throughout my many years at Luigi's, I have seen many people I've worked with leave and come back. They all realized they had an employer who recognized their self-worth, they felt accepted, and they felt they were a part of something great. They appreciated knowing they and their families were cared for. They recognized his equal compassion for them and the community we served, placing their needs before his own. I can remember a time where there was a regular customer and started having heart complications and couldn't come into the restaurant for a while. Your father had food sent to him and when he was finally able to dine at Luigi's again, he bawled tears of joy. He was so happy to be back at his favorite place and was so appreciative of the care and thoughtfulness of your father and many of the staff members. Actions like this are so rare to find in the workplace. Having a community led by someone who values their people like your dad does cannot fail."

Understanding the importance of internal communities, let us dive into the importance of external communities and how they affect each other. Having a healthy and stable internal community within your business is crucial to its long-term success. A perfect metaphor for this is when you're on an airplane and they instruct you in the occurrence of a plane wreck to apply your oxygen mask before helping others. If you and the members of your internal community aren't prepared and willing to help yourself and take the necessary actions to, how can you adequately help others?

Having a strong internal community with you and your staff aligned on the same goals and values best prepares you to sufficiently serve your external community. An external community is the people your business serves, as well as the community in which your business is geographically located. For example, our external community includes everyone that dines at our restaurant, anyone who enjoys Italian food, the town we are geographically located in, and every person and everything that embodies our town.

More importantly, when our internal community is healthy and vibrant, we are better suited to serve the needs of our external community. For example, when we take care of the needs of our staff, our business becomes a desirable place for people to work. When we are successful, we are better equipped to give back to our external community. We find ways to promote more commerce in the town. The more businesses that remain open in our town, the more people both locally and distantly will travel here, keeping it alive.

Long-time Clymer member, Robert Barto, has dedicated his time and his resources to the enhancement of the quality of life for Clymer and its residents. He served on council with my father for many years. When I asked Rob his opinion on how our business has contributed to our external community, he said, "Your dad has followed in his father's footsteps by becoming a public servant and proposing new ideas to the council. Ideas that would enhance the life quality of Clymer and the people of Clymer. One of my favorites is how he donated the plot of land (which he overpaid for) located between the two ball parks and worked with the council to receive a grant to build a veteran's memorial and civics park. This park now connects all our parks together, turning a vacant gravel lot into a beautiful contribution to the town."

He continued, "Aside from his contributions to the council, he has taken it upon himself to find other ways to keep a pulse in Clymer. If a building went up for sale, he'd figure out a plan for someone or something to reoccupy that building. In one of those buildings, he found an eye doctor and chiropractor to open offices in. Now our residents can walk to their doctor rather than drive to Indiana or somewhere else. He didn't have to do this, but he felt it was his civil duty as a local businessman to selflessly find ways to continually rejuvenate the town. Your dad and grandfather understood that any new business that opened in Clymer would benefit everybody."

Adding to this, Rob said, "In addition to this, he has always been willing to donate to the local schools, fundraisers, churches, local non-profits, The United Way, etc. Any organization that focused on serving the greater good of the community, both central to us and beyond he has been happy to do, and that says a lot. If there was someone down and out looking for work, your dad has always tried to find something for them so they could get some money in their pocket. It's clear he has a love for people and an appreciation for giving back to whoever he can, however he can."

He concluded, "One thing my wife and I agree on is that every time you walk into your restaurant, you feel like you belong. Your restaurant attracts people from all walks of life, and we witness you, your dad, and your staff treat every person like family. Your family and your staff make it a point to talk to all the customers, regardless of what they ordered. It's evident that you all care about not only your customers' experiences, but you care about their wellbeing. If there is someone in the community hosting a fundraiser, you and your team have been willing to contribute to the cause. If there was a customer who experienced a death in the family, your father and some staff were willing to attend their funeral service and oftentimes would donate food. You and your team care more about the lives of the people who patronize you more than what they spend."

Our values listed throughout this book are acted upon daily in the way we treat our patrons and our involvement in our local community, fulfilling our mission. Attending to the needs of our external communities has proven to us that long-term success is also dependent on using your resources in your internal community to benefit the external community at large. Below I have listed a few points on how building, sustaining, and maintaining a healthy internal and external community can benefit your businesses operations.

- They create awareness and lead to attract new customers. No better advertisement than positive word-of-mouth reviews, recommendations, and referrals.
- All your customers should be treated as if they are family or your favorite public figure. It is not common anymore for businesses to provide customer service that prioritizes the complete satisfaction and happiness of every single person that does business with you. Being treated as such undoubtable results in them returning to you again for your services, building a strong, loyal, and repetitive customer base.
- Collecting the feedback from your patrons is vital to the continuous improvement of the services you provide. Implementing a method to collect and respond to their feedback and using it to improve your services to better serve their needs also makes your patrons feel appreciated, heard, and recognized. They will appreciate your willingness to make operational changes that better equip you to serve their needs. One reason it is important to collect their feedback, opinions and ideas is because they view your business and services from an outsider perspective.
  - When you are a member of any business, you can innocently become blind to micro-level details that may stick out to others who do not visit your establishment or purchase your services on a daily basis. As I had mentioned before, life and circumstance constantly change. If you remain stuck in your ways

and live by the mentality "it has always worked and always will" you become susceptible to future failures, losing the competitive edge over your competitors.

- Supporting and giving back to the community you reside in pays huge dividends. Not only do you want them returning to your business, but it is also important to give back however and whenever you can with intentions of strengthening the prosperity of the town or city you reside in. Giving back shows that you care about your community and the people within it, and that you appreciate what they do to help support your business and the livelihoods of those who embody it.

CHAPTER 13

Call to Action

"I see no conflict whatsoever between Christianity and good business practices. People say you can't mix business with religion. I say there's no other way."

—S. TRUETT CATHY

This book was not written with the intent to showcase or brag about our successes in business. Rather, it was written with the intention of sharing with you the fundamentals of how long-term success in leadership is attainable despite any odds. I want to be clear about one thing: Our business is not perfect; we have our struggles, challenges, and let downs like every other business or organization. One thing I am clear about is this, we would not have been able to achieve what our business has in thirty-eight-plus years in a rural western Pennsylvania town with one red light if we didn't have strong values embedded into our business that we and our staff share in serving as our why—why we do what we do for a living and how doing it provides us the opportunity to better other people's lives. There have been many businesses or organizations that have come and gone. All of them differ in their physical reasons why, but the one thing most of them have in common is the lack of a strong set of values in their workplace culture.

Nothing in this world is perfect, and that's the way I believe our world was designed to be—not perfect. If everything in life was the way we wanted it, life would be boring. We would have nothing to look forward to, nothing to learn from, and nothing to help us grow or make us stronger. Nothing would give us a sense of fulfillment. Living in an imperfect world provides us humans with the opportunity to make it a little better for everyone. It provides us with the opportunity to learn from our mistakes and shortcomings and to use our free will to enhance the quality of our lives and others.

If you take one thing away from this book, I want you to develop a deeper understanding that success in business or leadership cannot be achieved alone. It requires an acknowledgment of your values. Your values fuel your beliefs and your actions. Leadership requires conducting your actions in a manner parallel to your values while building a team based on your values. It requires you to discard any self-benefitting goals and focus on how you and your business can benefit the greater good of both your internal and external communities. Staying consistent to this lifestyle will grant you and your business long-term success regardless of whatever challenges you may face. My family's business has been a testament to my claims, and I believe the information I share with you can help you and your business or organization accomplish the same thing.

This book has been methodically written in layers, all designed to highlight several important leadership traits in a new unique way. From a macro level or big-picture focus, the intention of this book is to draw a special focus to the importance of having strong values in the organization's culture and how having that will generate long-term success. Again, when we occupy a leadership position or create our own business, there are certain traits fueling our motives to take on this kind of challenge. Those traits are a direct reflection of our values.

Building a team composed of individuals who share in our values, goals, and mission propels the success of the business or organization, providing it with the resources it needs to not just survive, but continue to help the community at large however possible. In turn, the business or organization builds an unbreakable bond with the people they aim to serve. In leadership, if we take care of those who we lead, they will take care of us. When our team takes care of the needs of our community, our community remains loyal to our business for its services, thus fueling our success.

The micro level or more detailed focus of the book is how Benedictine Values are interrelated with necessary business leadership skills proven to be critical in ensuring long-term leadership and business success. It is commonly heard that as a business leader, you cannot mix business with religion. In some regards, it is logical not to. For example, as a business leader, it would not be considered ethical to force your employees or staff to believe in the same religion as you and practice that religion in the same way. It is illegal to discriminate against people who do not have religion or who have a different religion as you. We have not forced any of our staff or patrons to conform to our religious beliefs or values.

By highlighting how we use and live by Benedictine Values, my intentions were to show you, the reader, that you do not have to be a member of the Benedictine community or a denomination of Christianity to exercise these values and use them effectively. St. Benedict's viewpoint of these values go hand in hand with their broad definition, as well as show how that value is critical to success in leadership.

This is the first leadership development book showcasing how Benedictine Values are interrelated to business leadership skills and how they're critical for long-term success, backed by real life testimonies from individuals within the community the business serves and how those values have benefitted them, while providing readers with applicable methods on how an aspiring or current leader can implement these values into their businesses culture to ensure long-term success.

Whether a leader has a religious background or not, all leaders with short-term success and, more importantly, long-term success have exercised at least some if not all of these values. Think about it. Who would want to work for someone who doesn't treat you with dignity and worthiness? Something we all human beings are entitled to. Who wouldn't want a leader who takes time to reflect on who they are and who they aspire to be? That being a servant leader that cares about you and your success, as well and the business or organization you serve in? A leader mindful of their verbal and physical actions that affect how you feel and how you perform your job? Who wouldn't want to work in a stable work environment? Who wouldn't want to work for a leader who encourages daily conversion?

A leader who places an emphasis on working toward becoming your best self and is willing and able to help you achieve that? Who would want to work for a leader lacking the discipline to be obedient to the business or organization you serve in? Even through the hard or difficult times, who would want to work for someone that doesn't lead with humility and commitment to serving others? Who would want to work for a leader who isn't hospitable? Who doesn't make the initiative to welcome you by name, to ask you how you and your family are doing? That doesn't check to see if there is anything they can do to help you through tough times? Who doesn't greet you with a smile and is grateful for your contributions to their business or organization? Who would want to support a business or organization that neglects the needs of the community? That doesn't take time to give back to their staff or their community when the staff or community is in need?

The answer is quite simple. The individual would leave the organization and the community would no longer support it. You may have the most desired product on the market or the most efficient operations propelling your success in the short term, but if you do not have strong values embedded into the culture of your business (values such as these), it is inevitable that your business will not succeed in the long term.

My hope for this book is every reader in any leadership position, especially those who do not have a religious background, find a home for these Benedictine Values in your business or organization's culture. Whether you are in charge of a local non-profit, manage a restaurant, you're a teacher, or own your own business, my hope is this book will serve you as a toolkit, providing you with necessary leadership values proven to further develop your leadership skills while empowering and developing your followers into the best version of themselves they desire to be and the best person you need them to be.

I now challenge you, the reader, to go out into the world and try to make a difference however you can. First and foremost, remember to love others as yourself. Like the Beatles famously sang, "All we need is love." From true love of others as self, all these other values will flow naturally. Remember to take time for prayer, mindfulness, faithfulness, and reflection. We cannot grow into the person we aspire to be, nor can we encourage others to become who they desire to be if we do not take time to pray for the things we need and the things we're grateful for and remain mindful to the needs of others and our personal needs, stay faithful to your commitment to enhance the well-being of the greater good, and reflect on your actions and thoughts daily, using your reflections as benchmarks in your pursuit of becoming the person you want to become, and achieving the goals you set out to conquer.

Find a problem and create a stable solution to it. Never become content with, "We have always done things this way." Be willing to step out of your comfort zone, understand there is always room for improvement, and invite others to aid you in your initiatives to provide for the greater good. Do not allow yourself to become stagnant in life. Be willing to accept your mistakes, welcome your failures, and work toward becoming a better person. Allow yourself to take small steps and actions daily to convert you into the leader your community needs you to be. Inspire others to do the same; remain obedient to your team's and community's needs. When their needs are fulfilled, they will fulfill yours. Remain disciplined to the long-term goal. Do not give up in times of difficulty or failure. Recognize that difficulties arise in every facet of our lives. The sooner you accept that, the easier it will become to remain disciplined to your goals.

Show humility in your successes and your failures. Do not become boastful or conceited in your achievements. Be willing to give credit where credit is due and accept failure when you're at fault, even if you weren't directly involved. When you're a leader, you bear the responsibility of the actions of the people you lead. If you're in the position of leadership, you are not just called to lead, but to serve. Be a faithful steward to the needs of those whom your business or organization impacts. Be hospitable with everybody equally, regardless of their differences. Treat them with the equal human dignity and respect they deserve. We are all created equally, and as such, we should treat each other equally. Lastly, allow these actions to create the internal community your business needs to survive and in return, allow the success of your business to benefit the needs of your external community. Remember, without your external community, there is no internal community. Without a solid internal community, you will lose the support of your external community. From here, long-term success becomes attainable.

Thank you for reading *The Luigi Way: Benedictine Values Proven Effective in Leadership.* Go out and make a difference today. Amen.

Acknowledgments

If you read this entire book from the beginning to the end and have landed on this page, it is my honor to acknowledge you. It's been quite a challenging yet rewarding journey writing this book. If you were to ask me two years ago, it wouldn't have even crossed my mind. A conversation that planted the seed of authorship led to a sequence of divine intervention, allowing this idea to become a reality. The more I invested myself in writing this story, the more I realized the need for a unique book such as this.

In a world where we are told what to think and what to believe, I tried my best to write a book that allowed you, the reader, to think for yourself, to take stock of your own life, and to formulate your own opinions and interpretations of the literature I presented you with—book emphasizing the importance of having strong values in the workplace's culture to ensure long-term success, accompanied with real-life examples of how these Benedictine Values have aided our success serving as a case study, while providing you with an applicable way to instill these values into your leadership style as well as your workplace's culture.

My biggest accomplishment was sitting still long enough to put these thoughts in my head and into writing on my laptop. I have dedicated many, many hours to my writing. Each sentence has been meticulously thought out with the intention of providing you with a book that has both an interesting story with an applicable lesson. This process required me to dedicate time to being quieter and more absent than usual in the lives of loved ones. To all my friends and family who encouraged me in my writing process, edited my words, and edified my soul every step of this process, I am eternally grateful.

Dad, Mom, Angelica, and Sal. You have been my biggest supporters. You have supported me since the conception of this idea and continued to encourage me throughout the highs and lows of this journey. Thank you for dealing with me when I was stressed and pressed to meet deadlines, as well as sharing in my joy and excitement when I reached critical milestones. Thank you for always supporting me in everything I do. I am forever grateful and blessed to call you my family.

My amazing famiglia. Pictured from left to right is my father, my mother, Debi, me, my sister, Angelica, and my brother, Salvatore. Picture taken by one of our head servers, Madison Zometsky.

Aunt Mary, Paulette, Patricia, Vickie, Marilyn, Jeff, Shawn, Danny, and Shelby. Thank you for your countless years of devotion and commitment to Luigi's. Your input about your experiences of our workplace's culture featured in this book provides readers with a strong testament of what's possible when you have a dedicated team of individuals that share the same values and long-term goals. Your voices and your contributions further motivate me to be the best boss and leader I can be. My family and I are eternally grateful for you.

Scott, Dennis, Mary Beth, Debbie and Gerry, Kathleen and Bob, Rob, Joe and Marybeth, Mike and Diane, David, and Jeff and Linda. You all have been some of our most loyal patrons since our origins. Thank you for your continued friendships, support, and patronage. Your input about your customer service experiences provides a strong example to readers of what's possible when a business prioritizes the needs of their customers. My family, staff, and I are eternally grateful for you.

Alison Billon. Thank you for planting the seed in my head to write this book. Writing a book was something I never envisioned until you created the spark in me to pursue authorship. Thank you for believing that what our business stands for is something anyone in any form of leadership could benefit from. Your wisdom and compassion have benefited me since I first met you and became best friends with your son when we were four years old. I am eternally grateful for you, your family, and our friendship.

To the team at New Degree Press, thank you for allowing me to join your authorship program, providing a platform to bring my book to life. Eric Koester, Brian Bies, Jacqueline Claire Reineri Calamia, Linda Berardelli, and Cynthia Tucker deserve special thanks. No one has done more to make this book happen, though, than Jacqueline. Thank you for helping me build the foundation of my book, helping me develop its structure, and keeping me accountable so my manuscript was ready to be presented to NDP on time. Thanks for your patience, thoughtfulness, and close attention to detail.

This book was made possible by a community of people who believed in me so fervently they preordered their copies and helped promote the book before it even went to print. Thanks to you all, many of whom read my early manuscript and gave input on the book title and cover. You are amazing, and as promised, your name is rightfully printed in this book (listed in alphabetical order by first name):

Aaron Packer
AJ Dindinger
Alan Enterline
Alec Billon
Alex Domkowski
Alex Parkhurst
Alison Billon
Andrew Billon
Andrew Wetzel
Angela Lantzy
Angela Packer
Angela Streng
Annette Almes
Annette Martinage
Annie Rizzo
Anthony Frontino
Arthur J Dietz Jr
Austin Rauso
Bill Domkowski
Blake Shields
Brad Kluchurosky
Brad Remaley
Brandon Fandel
Brendan Shaughnessy
Bryan Martin
Carol Polenik
Channing Cavender
Cheri Jackel

Chloe DeFebo
Chris Cirillo
Christine Ferens Sciullo
Christine Walnoha
Christopher Zayachak
Claire Kirsch
Collin Hall
Colton Hearn
Courtney Patterson
Dan Dunchack
Danny Ferens
Dante Lombardi
Darcie Anselment
Darlene Rizzo
David Richard Ranieri
David T Bizousky
DeAnna Laverick
Debi Tate
Deborah Beisel
Deborah Frontino
Denise Packer
Dennis Previte
Diana Mervine
Diane & Mike Petras
Diane Waksmunski
Dino DeCario
Eden Bloom
Edward Kunz

Edward Tate
Edwin Camello
Elizabeth Wolfe
Eric Koester
Ethan Marshall
Frank Viggiano
Gabriella Bobak
Ganjofarid Anvarzod
Garrett Virostek
Gary Cary
Gerard Thomchick
Gianna Detore
Harley Walker
Jacquelyn McCarthy
James Buterbaugh
James Harvey
James Morley
Jamie Chichy
Janet Burkett
Jared Gregory
Jean Rellick
Jeffrey Zinkham
Jennifer Sleppy
Jennifer Watt
Jillian Butterworth
Joann M. Kujawa
Jodi Byers
Joe Marcoline
John C Hardesty Sr
John C. Tate
John Creps
John Henigin

John Marcius
John Michael Lucas
John Torres
Johnny Rizzo
Joseph Packer
Joshua McHarg
Julie C. Billon
Katrina McAfoos
Kelly Forrester
Kevin and Melissa Pritchard
Kimberly Woodley
Kimberly Sanchez
Kimberly Sobolewski
Kristen Robertson
Kristin Olsen
Lakeyn Semetosky
Lakyn Fornari
Laura Herrington
Laurie Sisk
Leonard Maliver
Libby Hinsley
Logan Lazor
Lori Creps
Louis Tate Sr.
Luke Anthony Walsh
Lupita Smith
Maddie Planinsek
Marcia Ann Croce
Marcy Wilson
Marilyn Haslego
Marshall Dietz
Martina Leonard

Mary Greb
Mary Roach
Mary Roland
Mary Tate
MaryBeth Campbell
Melissa Bender
Melissa Dunlap
Michael J. Grus
Michael Stahura
Michael Urick
Naomi Schwaiger
Nicholas Markovic
Nicole Wenturine
Nicolette Deyarmin
Patricia Pavlosky
Patrick & Amber Whitesel
Patrick Dougherty
Placid (Douglas) Sellers
Rachael Connor
Reid Brinkhoff
Rhonda Fiechuk
Rob Barto
Robert Allen Markley
Robert S. Dougherty
Russell Tate
Ryan Creps
Ryen Sawyer
Sandra H. Black
Sandra J Greene
Sarah Fiano
Scott Delauter
Selena Sleppy

Skip Spadafora
Steve Bivens
Steven Tate
Tammy Dalton
Teresa Tate Roumm
Theresa Crouse
Tina Busovicki
Tom Rusnock
William Hisker
William S Tate
Zach Fox
Zachary Hart
Zack Edgar

Appendix

———

INTRODUCTION

AJMC Staff. "A Timeline of COVID-19 Developments in 2020." AJMC. January 1, 2021. https://www.ajmc.com/view/a-timeline-of-covid19-developments-in-2020.

Avery Hartmans. "Roughly 17 Percent of US Restaurants Have Permanently Shut Down since the Start of the Pandemic as Industry Leaders Warn of an 'Unprecedented Economic Decline." *Business Insider*. December 7, 2020. https://www.businessinsider.com/thousands-us-restaurants-closed-coronavirus-pandemic-2020-12.

Kate Heinz. "Sixteen Signs of a Toxic Work Culture and How to Fix Them." Built In. October 17, 2021. https://builtin.com/company-culture/bad-company-culture.

Liz Ryan. "The Five Most Common Culture Problems—And Their Solutions." *Forbes*. August 13, 2016. https://www.forbes.com/sites/lizryan/2016/08/13/the-five-most-common-culture-problems-and-their-solutions/?sh=58fa4229bede.

Orderly. "Thirty-Five Reasons Why the Restaurant Failure Rate Is So High." Date accessed July 18, 2021. https://www.getorderly.com/blog/high-restaurant-failure-rate.

CHAPTER 2: MARCH 19, 2020 (WHEN COVID-19 RESTRICTIONS HIT HOME)

AJMC Staff. "A Timeline of COVID-19 Developments in 2020." AJMC. January 1, 2021. https://www.ajmc.com/view/a-timeline-of-covid19-developments-in-2020.

Avery Hartmans. "Roughly 17 Percent of US Restaurants Have Permanently Shut Down since the Start of the Pandemic as Industry Leaders Warn of an 'Unprecedented Economic Decline." *Business Insider.* December 7, 2020. https://www.businessinsider.com/thousands-us-restaurants-closed-coronavirus-pandemic-2020-12.

Christian Hetrick. "An Additional 2.4 Million Americans File for Unemployment, but Claims Drop in PA as Some Counties Reopen." *The Philadelphia Inquirer.* May 21, 2020. https://www.inquirer.com/economy/unemployment-benefit-claims-pennsylvania-coronavirus-20200521.html

Eric Rosenbaum. "America's Small Businesses Still Can't Find Workers, but That's Not Their Biggest Problem." CNBC. August 10, 2021. https://www.cnbc.com/2021/08/10/the-labor-shortage-isnt-main-streets-biggest-problem.html.

Greg Iacurci. "The 'Black Hole' of Unemployment Benefits: Six Months into the Pandemic, Some Are Still Waiting for Aid." CNBC. September 27, 2020. https://www.cnbc.com/2020/09/27/

why-some-states-are-struggling-to-pay-unemployment-bene-
fits.html.

National Restaurant Association. "100,000 Restaurants Closed Six
Months into Pandemic." August 17, 2021. https://restaurant.org/
news/pressroom/press-releases/100000-restaurants-closed-six-
months-into-pandemic.

Pennsylvania Government. "All Non-life-Sustaining Business in
Pennsylvania to Close Physical Locations as of 8 PM Today
to Slow Spread of COVID-19." March 19, 2020. https://www.
governor.pa.gov/newsroom/all-non-life-sustaining-business-
es-in-pennsylvania-to-close-physical-locations-as-of-8-pm-
today-to-slow-spread-of-covid-19/.

Tim Lambert. "When the State Stopped: A Look Back at How
Pennsylvania Arrived at a New Normal during the Coro-
navirus Pandemic." Witf. May 15, 2020. https://www.witf.
org/2020/05/15/when-the-state-stopped-a-look-back-at-how-
we-arrived-at-a-new-normal-during-the-coronavirus-pan-
demic/.

CHAPTER 3: LOVE YOUR NEIGHBOR AS YOURSELF

Bible Hub. "Genesis 1:27." Date accessed August 20, 2021. https://
biblehub.com/genesis/1-27.htm.

Darren J. Edwards Ph.D. "Learn to Love Yourself to Help You
Love Others." January 18, 2020. *Psychology Today.* https://www.
psychologytoday.com/us/blog/psychology-in-society/202001/
learn-love-yourself-help-you-love-others.

Dictionary.com s.v. "Leader." Date accessed August 20, 2021. https://www.dictionary.com/browse/leader.

Dictionary.com s.v. "Love." Date accessed August 20, 2021. https://www.dictionary.com/browse/love.

Ian Paul. "No, You Should Not Love Your Neighbor 'as You Love Yourself.'" Psephizo. April 27, 2020. https://www.psephizo.com/biblical-studies/no-you-should-not-love-your-neighbour-as-you-love-yourself/.

LMW. "The Golden Rule in Business." August 2, 2018. https://lmw.org/the-golden-rule-in-business/.

Robert K. Greenleaf Center for Servant Leadership. "What is Servant Leadership?" Date accessed August 20, 2021. https://www.greenleaf.org/what-is-servant-leadership/.

San Beda University. "The Ten Hallmarks of Benedictine Education." Date accessed February 15, 2022.https://www.sanbeda.edu.ph/posts/bmio/282/hallmarks-of-benedictine-education#:~:text=The%20Ten%20Hallmarks%20of%20Benedictine%20Education&text=The%20resulting%20collection%20of%20ten,of%20Benedictine%20Colleges%20and%20Universities.

Susan Bruno. "Five Ways to Practice Self-Love for Good Mental Health." The Transition House Inc. March 26, 2021. https://blog.thetransitionhouse.org/self-love-for-mental-health.

Thane Bellomo. "The Business of Leadership Requires Love." Talent Management. January 22, 2020. https://www.talentmgt.com/articles/2020/01/22/the-business-of-leadership-requires-love/.

The Christian Science Monitor. "'Love thy Neighbor as Thyself'—Is It Still Practical?" March 27, 2008. https://www.csmonitor.com/Commentary/A-Christian-Science-Perspective/2008/0327/p18s02-hfcs.html.

CHAPTER 4: PRAYER: A LIFE GUIDED BY MINDFULNESS, FAITHFULNESS, AND DEEP REFLECTION

Carla Naumburg. "Six Simple Steps to Being More Mindful." Seleni. March 21, 2018. https://www.seleni.org/advice-support/2018/3/21/6-simple-steps-to-being-more-mindful.

Dictionary.com s.v. "Faithfulness." Date accessed August 22, 2021. https://www.dictionary.com/browse/faithfulness.

Dictionary.com s.v. "Mindfulness." Date accessed August 22, 2021. https://www.dictionary.com/browse/mindfulness.

Dictionary.com s.v. "Reflection." Date accessed August 22, 2021. https://www.dictionary.com/browse/reflection.

Hisker, W.J. & Urick, M.J. 2019. Benedictine leadership. *Journal of Leadership and Management*, 15, 256-262.

Incredible One Enterprises. "Fifteen Scriptures That Entrepreneurs and Business Owners Should Leverage for Business Success." Date accessed August 22, 2021. https://incredibleoneenterprises.

com/15-scriptures-entrepreneurs-business-owners-lever-age-business-success/.

Lauren Abraham. "Weekly Devotional: Fruit of the Spirit—Faith-fulness." GCU. January 15, 2016. https://www.gcu.edu/blog/spiritual-life/weekly-devotional-fruit-spirit-faithfulness.

Marissa Levin. "Harvard Research Reveals How Mindful Leaders Develop Better Companies and Happier Employees." Inc. Date accessed August 22, 2021. https://www.inc.com/marissa-levin/harvard-research-reveals-how-mindful-leaders-develop-bet-ter-companies-happier-employees.html.

Merriam-Webster.com s.v. "Prayer." Date accessed January 23, 2022. https://www.merriam-webster.com/dictionary/prayer.

Palena Neale. "Self-Reflection in Leadership—Part One: Ambi-tions, Values, and Personality." Unabridged. February 19, 2019. https://unabridgedleadership.com/self-reflection-in-leader-ship/.

Theology of Work. "Faithful Leadership." Date accessed August 22, 2021. https://www.theologyofwork.org/the-high-calling/daily-reflection/faithful-leadership.

CHAPTER 5: STABILITY

Dictionary.com s.v. "Stability." Date accessed August 24, 2021. https://www.dictionary.com/browse/stability.

GitHub, Inc. "15.3 Characteristics of Organizational Culture." Date accessed August 24, 2021. https://saylordotorg.github.io/

text_organizational-behavior-v1.1/s19-03-characteristics-of-or-ganizatio.html.

Hisker, W.J. & Urick, M.J. 2019. Benedictine leadership. *Journal of Leadership and Management*, 15, 256-262.

Kate Eby. "Key Principles and How to Implement Them." Smart-sheet. October 11, 2019. https://www.smartsheet.com/content/operational-excellence.

Mary Juetten. "Failed Startups: Theranos." *Forbes*. December 13, 2018. https://www.forbes.com/sites/maryjuetten/2018/12/13/failed-startups-theranos/?sh=1b88562c5ca6.

Nawras Skhmot. "The Eight Wastes of Lean." The Lean Way. August 5, 2017. https://theleanway.net/The-8-Wastes-of-Lean#:~:-text=Lean%20thinking%20aims%20to%20remove,to%20understand%20what%20waste%20is.&text=The%20seven%20wastes%20are%20Transportation,by%20the%20acronym%20'TIMWOOD

Simplilearn. "What is Data Analysis: Methods, Process and Types Explained." December 31, 2021. https://www.simplilearn.com/data-analysis-methods-process-types-article.

Stella Maris College. "Benedictine Way of Life." Date accessed August 24, 2021. https://stellamaris.nsw.edu.au/wp-content/uploads/2015/06/benedictine-way-of-life.pdf.

CHAPTER 6: DAILY CONVERSION

Anne Tracy. "The Importance of Self-Improvement for Leaders." Illinois Leadership Center. Date accessed August 26, 2021. https://blogs.illinois.edu/view/8605/1833882347.

Beth Armknecht Miller. "Three Leadership Benefits of Self-Reflection." Executive Velocity. Date accessed August 26, 2021. https://executive-velocity.com/benefits-of-self-reflection/.

Life Coach Directory. "Judging Others—Is It Right or Wrong?" January 29, 2019. https://www.lifecoach-directory.org.uk/memberarticles/judging-others-is-it-right-or-wrong.

San Beda University. "The Ten Hallmarks of Benedictine Education." Date accessed February 15, 2022.https://www.sanbeda.edu.ph/posts/bmio/282/hallmarks-of-benedictine-education#:~:text=The%20Ten%20Hallmarks%20of%20Benedictine%20Education&text=The%20resulting%20collection%20of%20ten,of%20Benedictine%20Colleges%20and%20Universities.

WikiDiff. "Transformation vs. Conversion—What's the difference?" Date accessed August 26, 2021. https://wikidiff.com/transformation/conversion.

CHAPTER 7: OBEDIENCE

Bill Crawford. "Leadership: Influence vs. Obedience." Date accessed August 28, 2021. https://www.billcrawfordphd.com/leadership-influence-versus-obedience/.

Dictionary.com s.v. "Obedience." Date accessed August 28, 2021. https://www.dictionary.com/browse/obedience.

Hisker, W.J. & Urick, M.J. 2019. Benedictine leadership. *Journal of Leadership and Management*, 15, 256-262.

San Beda University. "The Ten Hallmarks of Benedictine Education." Date accessed February 15, 2022.https://www.sanbeda. edu.ph/posts/bmio/282/hallmarks-of-benedictine-education#:~:text=The%20Ten%20Hallmarks%20of%20Benedictine%20Education&text=The%20resulting%20collection%20of%20ten,of%20Benedictine%20Colleges%20and%20Universities.

CHAPTER 8: DISCIPLINE

Dictionary.com s.v. "Discipline." Date accessed August 30, 2021. https://www.dictionary.com/browse/discipline.

Hisker, W.J. & Urick, M.J. 2019. Benedictine leadership. *Journal of Leadership and Management*, 15, 256-262.

Journey to Leadership. "The Importance of Becoming a Self-Disciplined Leader." November 11,2019. https://journeytoleadershipblog.com/2019/11/11/importance-becoming-self-disciplined-leader/.

San Beda University. "The Ten Hallmarks of Benedictine Education." Date accessed February 15, 2022.https://www.sanbeda. edu.ph/posts/bmio/282/hallmarks-of-benedictine-education#:~:text=The%20Ten%20Hallmarks%20of%20Benedictine%20Education&text=The%20resulting%20collection%20

of%20ten,of%20Benedictine%20Colleges%20and%20Universities.

CHAPTER 9: HUMILITY

Assessment Systems. "The Importance of Humility in Leadership (Interview with Dr. Robert Hogan)." Date accessed September 1, 2021. https://asystems.as/the-importance-of-humility-in-leadership-interview-with-dr-robert-hogan/.

BibleGateway. "Luke 14:11. Luke 18:14." Date accessed September 1, 2021. https://www.biblegateway.com/passage/?-search=Luke+14%3A11%2CLuke+18%3A14&version=NIV.

Hisker, W.J. & Urick, M.J. 2019. Benedictine leadership. *Journal of Leadership and Management*, 15, 256-262.

John Baldoni. "Humility as a Leadership Trait." *Harvard Business Review*. September 15, 2009. https://hbr.org/2009/09/humility-as-a-leadership-trait.

Merriam-Webster. "Exalted". Date Accessed February 24, 2022. https://www.merriam-webster.com/dictionary/exalted.

Merriam-Webster. "Humility." Date Accessed February 24, 2022. https://www.merriam-webster.com/dictionary/humility.

Sherrie Campbell. "Nine Reasons Humility Is the Key Ingredient to Exceptional Leadership." Entrepreneur. August 24, 2017. https://www.entrepreneur.com/article/299140.

CHAPTER 10: STEWARDSHIP

Dictionary.com s.v. "Stewardship." Date Accessed September 3, 2021. https://www.dictionary.com/browse/stewardship.

Full Sail Leadership Academy. "Nine Essentials of Steward Leadership Development for Engaged Teams." August 12, 2020. https://fullsailleadership.com/9-essentials-of-steward-leadership-development-for-engaged-teams/.

Hisker, W. J. & Urick, M. J. 2019. Benedictine leadership. *Journal of Leadership and Management*, 15, 256-262.

Terri Kozlowski. "Compassion Is the Natural State of the Human Heart." October 27, 2020. https://terrikozlowski.com/compassion-is-human-nature/.

US Chamber of Commerce Foundation. "2019 Best Corporate Steward—Large Business Finalists." Date Accessed September 3, 2021. https://www.uschamberfoundation.org/2019-best-corporate-steward-large-business-finalists.

CHAPTER 11: HOSPITALITY

Courtney Capellan. "Hospitality Leadership—It's Not Just about Customer Service." About Leaders. October 1. 2015. https://aboutleaders.com/hospitality-leadership/#gs.czv8ua.

Dictionary.com s.v. "Hospitality." Date Accessed September 5, 2021. https://www.dictionary.com/browse/hospitality.

Hisker, W. J. & Urick, M. J. 2019. Benedictine leadership. *Journal of Leadership and Management*, 15, 256-262.

Hotel Business. "Adopt a Spirit of Hospitality for Long-Term Success." January 20, 2019. https://hotelbusiness.com/adopt-a-spirit-of-hospitality-for-long-term-success/.

Jan De Jonge. "The Importance of Hospitable Leadership in Hospitality." People Business Psychology. November 21. 2018. https://www.peoplebusinesspsychology.com/hospitable-leadership-in-hospitality/.

San Beda University. "The Ten Hallmarks of Benedictine Education." Date Accessed February 15, 2022.https://www.sanbeda. edu.ph/posts/bmio/282/hallmarks-of-benedictine-education#:~:text=The%20Ten%20Hallmarks%20of%20Benedictine%20Education&text=The%20resulting%20collection%20of%20ten,of%20Benedictine%20Colleges%20and%20Universities.

Sarah Anderson. "Five Keys to Successful Hospitality Leadership." School of Hospitality Administration Boston Hospitality Review. February 13, 2018. https://www.bu.edu/bhr/2018/02/13/5-keys-to-successful-hospitality-leadership/.

CHAPTER 12: COMMUNITY

David Spinks. "What If Your Business Is Actually a Community." Medium. September 13, 2016. https://medium.com/@davidspinks/what-if-your-entire-business-is-a-community-94c66e6e5bfc.

David Sprinks. "What's the Difference between Internal vs. External Communities?" Social Fresh. August 8, 2011. https://www.socialfresh.com/community-building-internal-external/.

Dictionary.com s.v. "Community." Date Accessed October 5, 2021. https://www.dictionary.com/browse/community.

Hisker, W.J. & Urick, M.J. 2019. Benedictine leadership. *Journal of Leadership and Management*, 15, 256-262.

John Allen. "Four Ways to Foster Great Employee Engagement." America's Charities. September 14, 2020. https://www.charities.org/news/4-ways-foster-great-employee-engagement?gclid=C-jwKCAjwzaSLBhBJEiwAJSRoktw-Jp4IorryyqtCcdZ8t5_lihE-sKJM1HUWEikZ7X_O4uS4Mm11zOhoCPXcQAvD_BwE.

Veronika Mazour. "Five Reasons Internal Communities Are Essential for Your Business." Exo. April 11, 2018. https://www.exoplatform.com/blog/5-reasons-internal-communities-es-sential-business/.

Made in the USA
Middletown, DE
28 October 2023

41390637R00129